At Moments for Moms, we believe that every mother's journey is a story worth telling. Our mission is to empower mothers to embrace their unique experiences, preserve their legacies, and create meaningful impact in their families and communities. Through storytelling, mentorship, and faith-driven encouragement, we provide a space for moms to share their wisdom, find support, and leave a lasting imprint for generations to come.

We are a community for:

Mothers of All Backgrounds – Whether you're a new mom, a seasoned mother, or a grandmother, your journey matters.

Women with a Story to Tell – If you've faced challenges, overcome obstacles, and want to share your wisdom, this is your platform.

Faith-Driven Moms – We uplift and support mothers who desire to grow spiritually while nurturing their families.

Legacy Builders – Those who want to document their journey and pass down invaluable lessons to future generations.

Moments for Moms IV Inspiration and Wisdom for Every Season of Motherhood

VISIONARY: Juanita N. Woodson
CO-AUTHORS:

Crystal D. Harrison M.Ed.
Dr. Tanisha Tyler Graves
Paula Banks
Joi West Phalo
Dani Nicole
Sabrina Clemons
Dr. Tiffany Sayles
LaQuana Dena Wigfall
Dr. Nikki Lawrence
Cheryl Lynne
Stephanie Wills
Lillian Jackson
Valencia Franklin
Devon Garrison
Terrie Ann Polk
Dr. Yulanda Dante' West
Tonisha Morton
Jvonne Belle
Ebony Bailey
Debbie Luckett

Moments for Moms IV: Inspiration and Wisdom for Every Season of Motherhood
Copyright © 2025 by Juanita N. Woodson,
Crystal D. Harrison M.Ed., Dr. Tanisha Tyler Graves, Paula Banks
Joi West Phalo, Dani Nicole, Sabrina Clemons, Dr. Tiffany Sayles,
LaQuana Dena Wigfall, Dr. Nikki Lawrence, Cheryl Lynne, Stephanie
Wills, Lillian Jackson, Valencia Franklin, Devon Garrison, Terrie Ann
Polk, Dr. Yulanda Dante' West, Tonisha Morton, Jvonne Belle, Ebony
S. Bailey, Debbie Luckett

Published by Grace 4 Purpose, Publishing Co. LLC
ISBN: 979-8-9926893-9-6
Editing by: Grace 4 Purpose, Publishing Co. LLC
Book cover design by Grace 4 Purpose, Publishing Co. LLC
Printed and bound in the United States of America

Dedication

This book is dedicated to you, Mama.

In the sleepless nights, in the long days, and in the moments that feel both overwhelming and beautiful, may these words remind you that you are not alone. Your love matters. Your sacrifices matter. *You* matter.

As you turn these pages, may you find encouragement for your weary days, joy for your heart, and wisdom for every season of motherhood. May you be reminded that your journey is significant, your voice is powerful, and your presence is irreplaceable.

This is for you—the mother who continues to show up with faith, grace, and love.

With love and gratitude,
The Authors of *Moments for Moms Volume IV*

Table of Contents

Table of Contents

"When life feels heavy, remember: you were chosen, for this season."

MOMENTS FOR MOMS
Introduction

Motherhood is one of God's greatest callings. It is a journey that stretches us, grows us, and draws us closer to Him. From sleepless nights and toddler giggles to teenage milestones and the quiet wisdom of later years, every season of motherhood carries both challenges and blessings. Yet through it all, God's presence is constant, reminding us that we do not walk this journey alone.

"She is clothed with strength and dignity; she can laugh at the days to come." — Proverbs 31:25

Moments for Moms Volume 4 was created to encourage you in those very moments—both the joyful and the difficult. Inside, you will find personal testimonies, reflections of faith, and wisdom born from real-life experiences. Each story is a reminder that your role as a mother is purposeful, your sacrifices are seen by God, and your love leaves an eternal impact.

As you read, may you be refreshed and uplifted. May you be reminded that your strength is not found in perfection but in God's grace. May these pages give you hope for today and courage for tomorrow, knowing that the One who entrusted you with this calling also equips you for it.

"He tends his flock like a shepherd: He gathers the lambs in his arms and carries them close to his heart; he gently leads those that have young." — Isaiah 40:11

Welcome to Moments for Moms Volume 4. May this book be a source of strength, inspiration, and a gentle reminder that you are seen, valued, and deeply loved—by your children, by those around you, and most importantly, by God.

"When you set boundaries with grace, you teach your children the language of honor."

MOMENTS FOR MOMS

Chapter One
Minister Dr. Tanisha Tyler Graves
Without Boundaries, There is No Respect

Typically, what separates a child from a parent is that former the hasn't been to the places emotionally that the latter has. Mind you, I said *typically.* The world in which we live in has changed dramatically over time, so my initial statement may no longer be definitive or totally accurate.

Now, what I am about to share with you is not a lesson I learned overnight. I was a young mother—learning and maturing while on the job. I didn't have all the answers, and oftentimes, I pretended I did so that outsiders would not question my competence as a mom or my ability to care for those I loved most.

Who are we as people, and why do we live the way that we do? Why are parents commissioned to lead and children commanded to follow? Biblically, there are no scriptures that dictate parents cannot be friends with their children. Ideally, you want to be approachable—because if a child is uncomfortable coming to you with a problem, they will seek out a resolution somewhere else, often from an outlet that does not have their best interests at heart.

Of the 613 commandments listed in the Old Testament alone, God made sure that one of the most important—given to Moses and included in the initial Ten—was the fifth: *"Honor your father and your mother."*

Children imitate what they see. Biblically, an onus—a responsibility— is placed on parents to lead, guide, and offer the necessary supervision to ensure that their children are walking in the ways of the Lord. If not the parents, then who?

But child, how am I going to teach you the ways of the Lord—physically, spiritually, and emotionally—if I think like a child and lead as a child? This is a great example of the blind leading the blind.

Mama, just as Moses was given the Ten Commandments from the Lord to deliver to the Israelites, we too must share God's commandments with our children. God set boundaries so that both parents and children could follow. He laid the foundation and established those boundaries. Without boundaries, we are easily pressured or influenced to do wrong and commit sins that God has commanded us not to do.

Keep the laws of God above all things and remember this:
"Without boundaries, there is no respect."

Rules are put in place to maintain decency and order—a blueprint or code of conduct to ensure that generational blessings continue while generational curses cease.

The young Apostle Timothy was transparent in his second epistle, explaining why the Gospel was given, its relevance, and how obedience to one's Heavenly Father would set an example and combat all of the issues troubling humanity both then and now.

As one takes a look at the plight of humanity so eloquently described by Timothy, the images and the deep concern for our youth growing up in such a time as this are beyond terrifying.

2 Timothy 3:1–5 warns us of these times, and reading Paul's words to Timothy hit me hard—he described the very world our children are growing up in today. That's when I knew: *Parenting without God's Word isn't just hard—it's dangerous.*

In verses 12–17, Paul goes on to explain and encourage:

"These passages give wise counsel to live a God-filled life, being obedient to His Word and turning away from that which is wrong—this equips us for good works."

The Word of God Provides Instructions

Mama, say it with me:
"Without boundaries, there is no respect!"

There's a reason why mama is not your friend—because she doesn't want your safety or your salvation compromised! Both mean far more than an emphatic social media endorsement or validation as an "exceptional mother" in front of your friends.

You see, God commands us to *"Train up a child in the way he should go, and when he is old, he will not depart from it"*(Proverbs 22:6).

Invest your time, effort, and patience into your children. As a Christian mother, incorporate the principles and attributes required by God—

known as the *Fruits of the Spirit*: love, joy, peace, longsuffering, gentleness, goodness, faith, meekness, and temperance.

Why am I doing this while also being mindful of my own actions? Because I'm not only teaching my son or daughter obedience, but also the benefits and consequences of compliance and defiance. I'm training them with the hope of a desired outcome—an expectation—that they will pass these same values down to my grandchildren and great-grands.

And yes, as a mother and grandmother, it is my job to be prepared when they come to me and ask, "Why must I do things this way?" Instead of simply saying, "Because I said so," I must teach them *why*.

Even when your children get upset with you for disciplining them, let them know they may not understand now, but they will as they get older.

When my children were young, I always let them know they could come talk to me about anything. There was no conversation off-limits. Sometimes I lacked patience when they didn't do what I told them, and yes, it upset me—but that never stopped them from talking to me.

Even as adults, they try their best not to curse or raise their voices when angry. If they ever say something disrespectful in anger, they come back and apologize. That respect was built through boundaries.

They have never allowed their peers to speak disrespectfully to their parents, and that still stands today. **Set those boundaries while they are young, and as adults, your children will respect you.**

What My Children Taught Me About Boundaries

1. The child will appreciate you.
2. They will show respect in how they speak and treat you.
3. As children, they may think you're tough—but as parents themselves, they will understand your wisdom.

4. They will trust you to continue guiding them as adults because of the example you set early on.

A Mother's Prayer

"Lord, help me parent with purpose. Give me the wisdom to recognize when my children are in trouble, to discipline when correction is needed, and to lead by example. Help me set boundaries with boldness, even when it hurts. God, grant me the serenity to accept the things I cannot change, the courage to change the things I can, and the wisdom to know the difference. My goal is their growth—not their comfort."

A Prayer of Gratitude

Father God, thank You for creating me as Your authoritative voice to raise and lead my children. For I know that if it had not been for You on my side, the world would have taken my children, leaving them to wander in darkness and live a life filled with sin. But to God be the glory—my children know You in the pardon of their sins and are striving to live righteous lives. **Amen.**

Deuteronomy 6:6–7 (NIV):

"These commandments that I give you today are to be on your hearts. Impress them on your children. Talk about them when you sit at home and when you walk along the road, when you lie down and when you get up."

Final Word to Mothers

Mama's, be a parent first—and remember:
Without Boundaries, There Is No Respect!

Pause & Reflect: Setting
Boundaries in Love

Dr. Minister Tanisha Tyler Graves

Minister Dr. Tanisha Tyler-Graves is a nationally recognized health educator, advocate, and entrepreneur whose mission is to educate and raise awareness about the stigma surrounding epilepsy. She dedicates her time, talent, and resources to working alongside vulnerable populations to improve their social, economic, and health outcomes.

She collaborates closely with a wide range of stakeholders, including faith-based ministries, veterans, and parents of children with disabilities such as epilepsy and rare diseases.

A sought-after speaker, presenter, and panelist, Tanisha is also a proud wife, mother, grandmother, and civic leader. She and her husband, Bobby, work tirelessly to amplify the voices of those advocating for health, economic, and social equity—especially those often excluded from decision-making tables.

Minister Dr. Tyler-Graves is the founder of two nonprofit organizations: **Operation Love, Inc.** (serving the underserved) and **When the Trumpet Sounds** (advocating for the epilepsy community). She will complete her Doctorate in Biblical Counseling in 2025 and is also a certified seizure instructor and an alumna of the F.B.I. Citizens Academy.

In addition, Minister Tyler-Graves serves as a consumer reviewer for the federal government, critiquing grants related to epilepsy, seizures, and traumatic brain injury. In this role, she reviews studies for potential funding and evaluates medical devices prior to their release into the community.

She was honored as **Ambassador of the Month** for both February and July 2022 by the Danny Did Foundation.

An accomplished author, she is the writer of *I Pulled the Sun Out for You* and a three-time best-selling co-author featured in *Moments for Moms, Volumes II & III,* and *Faith While Waiting.*

Contact Information

Website:
TanishaTylerGraves.com
Wtts4epilepsy.org
Operationloveinc.org
Facebook: Tanisha Graves

"There is beauty in the woman who still believes after being broken."

MOMENTS FOR MOMS

Chapter Two
Paula Banks
The Love I Didn't Think I Deserved

For the Woman Who Thought Love and Motherhood Weren't Meant for Her

I spent a long time convinced that I wasn't made for motherhood. Not because I didn't love children but because I was terrified of loving someone so deeply and then losing them. That kind of love felt too risky. My own father had been absent from my life, and the silence he left behind echoed louder than any words he could have said.

That abandonment shaped how I saw the world and how I saw myself. I told people I didn't want kids, but the truth was, I didn't think I could handle the responsibility of raising someone when I was still carrying so much pain of my own. I feared I would pass on what I hadn't healed.

Abandonment does something to you, especially to a girl whose only wish was to be a daddy's girl. It breaks you in quiet, invisible ways. I remember watching other girls be loved by their fathers, picked up, hugged tightly, told they were beautiful. I'd watch from the outside looking in, silently wondering what that kind of love must feel like. Every night, I prayed to God for a dad. Not even necessarily my biological one, just someone who would choose me and love me like I was his. But when it didn't happen, I gave up asking, I figured maybe God had skipped over that prayer.

Looking back, I realize He never skipped it. He was holding it saving it for a time when I could understand what restoration truly looked like.

"The Lord is close to the brokenhearted and saves those who are crushed in spirit." (Psalm 34:18)

 That was me. Crushed by what I didn't get. Convinced I was unworthy of what I now know was never too late to receive.

The Shift I Didn't Expect

I wasn't searching for love when I met my husband. In fact, I had already made peace with the idea that love, at least the lasting kind, just wasn't in the cards for me. I had learned to expect people to leave. So when he came into my life, so kind, so sure, and so consistent, I didn't trust it. I gave him grief. I fought him every step of the way, not out of spite, but out of fear. He was too good to be true, and I didn't believe something that steady could possibly be meant for me.

But he stayed. Through the walls I built, the questions I threw at him and the messiness I couldn't hide. He didn't try to rescue me or fix me, he simply stood beside me and loved me through it and one day, something inside me softened. I began to believe him not just his words, but the way he saw me. As someone worthy, capable, someone who could be a mother not in spite of her past, but because of the healing she had walked through.

He made it clear from the beginning that he wanted a family. I laughed it off, thinking there was no way I could be someone's mother. But somehow, God was using him to show me a new version of myself one I had never allowed myself to imagine.

When I found out we were pregnant with our first son, my heart jumped but so did my stomach. I remember sitting on the edge of the tub, holding the test like it might disappear if I blinked too long. There it was. Clear as day. Positive. I stared at that little plastic stick, barely breathing. I was going to be someone's mother.

The excitement was real, but so was the fear. Not the kind that screams, it whispered. It crept in slowly, in between the congratulations. It sounded like: Will I know how to love him the right way? What if I mess this up? What if he grows up with questions I can't answer and pain I didn't mean to pass down?

During my pregnancy, I was so afraid that I wouldn't have that motherly instinct. It kept me up at night. I'd lay there in the dark, my hand resting on my belly, wondering if I'd know what to do when the time came. I worried that the instinct I inherited wouldn't be the one to nurture but the one to abandon. The fear that I'd disappear emotionally the way my father did haunted me. I remember praying hard for God to break that pattern. I asked Him not to let me repeat what had hurt me.

I didn't want to be the one to mess this up. My child deserved two parents present, loving, and fully engaged. I didn't want to be the reason that dream cracked. That pressure was real, and it pressed down on my chest some nights until the tears came without warning.

But even in that space, God was gentle and offered presence. That presence came through my husband's patience, soft whispers in prayer and the quiet ways I began to see myself differently. I was being reshaped not by fear, but by love. A love that held space for my pain without letting it lead.

As my belly grew, so did my courage. I started talking to God more honestly, I started letting my husband love me without deflecting. I began to understand that healing doesn't mean all the pain is gone, it means you're no longer afraid to live fully despite it.

Motherhood didn't make me whole, but it revealed that I already had the pieces I just needed to believe they belonged to me. I was already capable, already worthy and already chosen.

I learned that healing didn't have to be finished before love showed up. God sent someone who saw the broken places in me and didn't flinch.

"See, I am doing a new thing! Now it springs up; do you not perceive it?" (Isaiah 43:19)

 I didn't see it at first, but God was already planting something new, even when I thought my story was stuck in survival. He was making his way in the wilderness; he was restoring what I thought I had missed.

To the mother who feels forgotten, unworthy, or left behind I want you to know that none of those things are true. You are not disqualified because of your past. You are not too late, too broken, or too far gone. The love you didn't believe in might be the love God is preparing for you right now.

Redemption is still possible and the story you never imagined living might be the exact one God had in mind all along.

If you've spent years convincing yourself that love and motherhood weren't meant for you, know that rewriting that belief takes time, but it's possible. That shift doesn't come from forcing yourself to "get over "your past. It comes from slowly letting in the truth that you care not too broken, too late, or too far gone to experience love; real love and to give it.

Here are a few ways that helped me, and may help you too:

- **Start with your own reflection**. Some days, I had to look into the mirror and say out loud, "I am worthy of love," even when I didn't believe it. Over time, the words became softer to say, and the truth began to settle in.
- **Notice where love is already present.** It might not look like the picture you imagined, but it's there, in the friend who checks on you, the child who runs into your arms, or even the way you care for yourself on hard days.
- **Let yourself receive.** If you've been in survival mode, it's easy to deflect kindness with "I'm fine" or "You don't have to." Practice saying "Thank you" and letting people show up for you without explaining it away.
- **Mother from the heart you have now.** You don't need a perfect history to be the mother your child needs. You need presence, honesty, and the courage to keep showing up.

Love is not something you have to earn by "doing better" or "being more". It is something you were created for. You were always meant to have it. Even if you've told yourself otherwise.

Your story doesn't disqualify you from love, it deepens your capacity to give it. The day you start to believe that is the day you step fully into the life you were meant to live.

Restored by Love: My Reflection

Paula Banks

Paula Banks is the CEO and Founder of EION Books, a creative education and publishing house shaping how stories are taught, told, and passed down. Through her signature programs LitKids Create and Story Hustle, she equips parents, educators, and young authors with tools to nurture confident storytellers and learning experiences grounded in representation and creative expression. Her work blends storytelling, education, and legacy amplifying diverse voices and reminding families that storytelling isn't just about writing books; it's about building the future.

Contact Information

Social Media:
@authorpaulabanks
Website: Eionbooks.com
Email:
Contact@paulaybanks.com

"The storms you survive become the strength your children stand on."

MOMENTS FOR MOMS

Chapter Three
Dani Nicole
Walking Through the Storm with Joy and
Resilience

"And we know that in all things God works for the good of those who love him, who have been called according to his purpose".
(Romans 8:28)

Still, I Rise – Moving in your God Given Purpose

Maya Angelo an American poet, memoirist, civil rights activist, and performer has written many poems, but one poem stands out the most to me and that's *"Still I Rise."* Taking one passage that reads: *"Just like moons and like suns, With the certainty of tides. Just like hopes springing high, Still I Rise.*

Have you experienced a period in your life where the challenges seemed like more than you could bear? Was it difficult to rise to the occasion? If so, how did you rise above it?

As a single mother, there were days when the weight of responsibility felt almost unbearable and every dollar stretched felt like a small victory against defeat. There were late nights spent wondering how I would keep the lights on or put food on the table, but I refused to let my children sense the fear and anxiety that threatened to overwhelm me. Instead, I gathered every ounce of courage and hope, holding tight to the conviction echoed in Maya Angelou's words—that no matter the darkness or uncertainty, I would rise. That promise to myself became my anchor, reminding me that even in my loneliest moments, I possessed a strength that could not be extinguished.

There were moments when reality struck hard—my income was just above the threshold for food assistance or, at one stressful juncture, I was unable to qualify for health insurance. The disappointment and frustration were overwhelming, and at times I felt invisible to a system that overlooked those who struggle in silence. Yet, during discouragement, I clung to a quiet hope, telling myself the hardship was only temporary. I drew on every ounce of faith and determination, trusting that—even through the darkest nights—I would find the strength to rise above and overcome these challenges.

In the past year, I found myself standing at a crossroads of self-reflection, forced to face the swirling storm of my emotions, thoughts, and behaviors, and to finally acknowledge the triggers that left me feeling raw and exposed. Earlier in my journey as a mother, I barely had time to catch my breath; every day felt like a race against exhaustion and worry, and self-reflection was a luxury I could not afford. I was desperately treading water, hoping not to go under while carrying the weight of responsibility and fear. I missed the moments to slow down, to listen to my heart, to ask myself what truly hurt and what I truly needed. At times, I experienced sadness, consumed by anger, or haunted by doubt about my abilities. Yet, it was only when life demanded I pause and look inward that I began to see those feelings not as weaknesses, but as signposts, guiding me toward healing and strength.

As I turned inward for self-reflection, a wellspring of raw emotion surfaced—grief, gratitude, fear, and hope swirling within me, demanding to be felt and understood. The journey toward self-awareness became not just an intellectual exercise, but an act of courage, a daily practice of facing the truth of my heart. I began to recognize, sometimes with tears streaming down my face, the weight my thoughts and feelings carried and how deeply they influenced my actions, my standards, and the way others perceived me.

There were moments of profound vulnerability, when understanding myself felt overwhelming, but also moments of unexpected grace, when I chose gentleness over judgment. As I continued this path of growth, I realized I needed to extend the same emotional insight and compassion to my child—learning to recognize their silent signals, their fears, and their hopes, just as I was learning to interpret my own.

Reflecting on the first fifty years of my life was not just an exercise in memory; it was a journey through waves of longing, regret, pride, and deep, abiding love. With every honest reckoning, I gained a richer understanding of who I truly am and what my spirit longs for most, emerging with a sense of purpose and a heart that, despite everything, still dares hope.

Looking back now, a surge of gratitude mixed with bittersweet relief as I realize how necessary those turbulent emotions, thoughts, and behaviors truly were. They became the compass guiding me through storms of doubt and sorrow in a place where fear of losing relationships, fear of rejection—no longer held me captive. Instead, I discovered new depths of courage and self-acceptance, sometimes through tears and sometimes through fierce determination. I know now that every struggle was shaping me into someone who would never again allow uncertainty to dictate my path.

I strive each day not only to do my best, but to finally feel worthy of the joy and hope that life has to offer. With that realization came the difficult but empowering decision to distance myself from people, places, and situations that dimmed my spirit. In letting go, my heart aches and then soars—I am finally moving forward, believing I deserve all the good and all the healing that is to come.

It is natural to feel the weight of waiting for the right moment and to wonder if hope will ever break through the clouds of uncertainty. When you are overwhelmed, give yourself grace to pause and gently reflect on which parts of your life could shift, even if only a little. Sometimes, the barriers we battle are not just around us, but within us—old fears, doubts, or heartaches that whisper their limits. Embracing responsibility for your own journey, though daunting, is a profound act of courage and self-love.

Faith, too, can feel fragile in the hardest seasons—a flicker in the dark. But let that small spark be enough. Like scripture says, even faith as small as a mustard seed can move mountains. Let your faith become movement: a whispered prayer, a careful step forward, a brave decision to try again. Trust that your actions, guided by hope and belief in your own resilience, will draw you toward brighter days.

I can do all things through Christ who strengthens me.
(Philippians 4:13)

You are not alone—truly, so many mothers know the ache and exhaustion of carrying burdens that sometimes feel too heavy. If you are reading this, I hope you feel seen and understood. Let your heart take comfort in knowing that, even on your hardest days, resilience and hope live within you. Lean into your faith, even if it feels fragile, and trust that you possess a deep well of strength and courage, ready to carry you through.

Every mother is worthy of compassion, healing, and joy. You have the power to rise again, no matter how many times you stumble. Know that your struggles do not define you; rather, they are shaping you into someone more luminous and braver. Moms, you are valued and never truly alone on this journey.

Lord, with a heart full of thanksgiving, I pray that every woman reading this feels Your loving presence wrapping around her. May she sense the truth of her worth and the strength You have placed deep within her spirit. Let her know that even in her most fragile moments, she is never alone, you see her, cherish her, and walk beside her through every trial. Grant her courage to rise when she feels weak, faith to believe when doubt clouds her mind, and the comfort of knowing that Your love will never let her go. **Amen**

Walking Through the Storm: My Reflection

....

....

....

....

....

....

....

....

....

....

....

....

Dani Nicole

Dani Nicole is a best-selling author, mentor, and speaker who seeks to leave a legacy as a writer who dared to be fearless, carved light out of darkness, and gave readers permission to believe in love, resilience, and themselves.

In 2024, she released her first solo novel, *Entangled with Deceit*, and has since contributed to two anthologies—*Moments for Moms, Volumes 3 & 4*. Born in Milwaukee, Wisconsin, Dani now resides in Charlotte, North Carolina, with her youngest son.

From a young age, writing has been her passion and her outlet. Her motivation stems from the stories within her that refuse to stay silent.

Dani writes to heal, to hope, and to breathe—both for the woman she once was and for those who need to hear her words today.

Contact Information

Website:
www.payhip.com/TheVarietyShop
Facebook: Dani Nicole
Instagram: @daninicoleauthor
Linktree: https://linktr.ee/dnhall

"The same grace that covers your children covers you too."

MOMENTS FOR MOMS

Chapter Four
Sabrina Clemons
Grace for the Chosen

"I give grace because I so desperately need it." – *Lysa Terkeurst*

Moms are chosen and so are their children. We are not here by accident. We were all in the mind of God when He created the earth. He created each of us with a purpose. This is something that we all should always remember, especially through the ups and downs of life. We all need the reminder. It's a truth that strengthens us in moments of weakness and weariness. Where I am weak, He is strong. You are not in this alone. Grace supplies the power to keep going. It's the wind in your back that says, *Don't stop. Keep going. You can do this*

His Grace is sufficient and it's part of His plan. Biblically, grace is defined as the unmerited favor and love God shows toward mankind. It's not earned through works. Grace draws us closer to God and reminds us of our dependence on Him. It is His kindness and favor that gives us peace and hope.

Although there are many definitions of grace, one that also applies to moms is the *quality or state of being considerate or thoughtful*. From the beginning, grace was extended, first to Adam and Eve. Even though they failed, God's love covered them. Grace gave them another chance. As mothers, grace is both the gift we receive and the gift we must keep giving, especially to our children. They make mistakes, but so do we. They aren't perfect and neither are we. We don't always make the best decisions, but the grace of God covers us even then.

2 Corinthians 12:9 states, *"My grace is sufficient for thee: for my strength is made perfect in weakness."*

This verse reminds us that God's grace is enough to support us, especially in our weakness. His divine strength is most evident when we are vulnerable. It serves as a reminder that challenges can lead to spiritual strength and growth as we rely on God's power.

We All Have Challenges

Our story will always include challenges, but triumph is in our view, for us and for our children. God chose us to steward them through every age and stage of life. Why stewardship? He has a plan for their lives too, and He trusts us with this assignment. What an honor and a privilege to be chosen.

As a mother of two young adults, it's sometimes a challenge to remember to give grace—especially when I don't understand or agree with their decisions. But grace creates the space needed for understanding. It opens a path to be heard. It allows our children to walk through an open door and still be embraced and loved no matter what they've done.

I've learned that it's better to provide what I call a *"grace space"* than to judge them based on my own opinions. In that space, they know they can share what's on their heart and feel safe doing it. I listen, and if they're open, I offer sound advice. I cherish those moments because that same space gives me the chance to share my heart with them too. Believe it or not, grace goes both ways—the space you give is often the space you get back.

As moms, we carry our own personal struggles, the ones we rarely talk about—especially with our children. But even in those moments, we have to remember it's okay to give *ourselves* grace. Sometimes the challenges we face make us question our parenting or the decisions we're making in life, and that can stir up feelings of inadequacy. But even then, we have to hold tight to the truth that God chose us for this role. He didn't call the equipped; He equips the called.

I Am Still Chosen

I know the plans for you, Jeremiah 29:11 says. We have heard this scripture many times before;
For I know the plans I have for you," declares the Lord, "plans to prosper you and not to harm you, plans to give you hope and a future.
(KJV)"

This scripture reminds us that God's intentions toward us are good. He offers guidance and care, assuring us that we are not alone.

As mothers, the struggle is real. We are not perfect, but we are still chosen. The Bible shows many mothers raising children—such as Jochebed, mother of Moses; Elizabeth, mother of John the Baptist; and Mary, mother of Jesus. They weren't perfect, women, but they were available. God chose them before time to bring forth some incredible offsprings that would impact the world and be forever stamped in History. Let that sink in. You and your children are called to greatness regardless of imperfections!

Grace Extended

During weak or difficult times, extend grace to yourself.

1. **Mindset:** Remember that you are chosen
2. **Sight:** Ask God to help you see yourself as He sees you.
3. **Allowance:** Give yourself room to make mistakes. Forgive yourself and keep moving.
4. **Love:** Love yourself. Receive the love you freely give to others.

Grace is the gift that keeps us grounded on this journey in motherhood.

Affirmations for the Chosen

As you embrace your chosen journey, continue to affirm yourself:
1. I am chosen for such a time as this.
2. I am embracing my unique journey of grace.
3. I will be gentle with myself, knowing I am doing my best.
4. I can do all things through Christ, who strengthens me.
5. It is through His sufficiency that I am strengthened to be efficient!

Other famous quotes to live by:

1. "Forgive yourself for not knowing what you didn't know before you learned it." – Maya Angelou
2. "Loving yourself isn't vanity. It's sanity." – Katrina Mayer
3. "When grace moves in… guilt moves out." – Max Lucado
4. "Talk to yourself like someone you love." – Brené Brown
5. "Grace means that all of your mistakes now serve a purpose instead of serving shame." – Mike Rusch

Grace for the Called: My Reflection

....

....

....

....

....

....

....

....

....

....

....

....

Sabrina Clemons

Sabrina L. Clemons is a kingdom-minded woman of faith with a kingdom assignment. Her purpose is to be about her Father's business bringing glory to Him in everything she does, while speaking truth in love, life and healing, and the oracles in which the Father reveals and chooses her to speak. Ordained and consecrated in 2006, she has led several teams in the ministry over the years. She has also served as a Church Administrator, and in the role of Co-Pastor while her husband led Resurrection House International Ministries.

Currently, her assignment in the marketplace ministry is serving and leading as a regional director for a nonprofit organization and she is the founder of a budding ministry - Rising from the Ashes. She is dedicated and provides services that stimulate and enhance growth, development, and solutions for mind, soul and spirit, while advancing the kingdom agenda.

Sabrina L. Clemons is a graduate of Norfolk State University and continued her graduate studies at Hampton University. Additionally, she continued her ministry studies through the Freedom (Life) School of Ministry, and currently through Eagles International Training Institute and The Truth in the Spirit Priesthood Academy. She is a contributing author in the books 'Hear Me Roar' and 'The Traits of Women of Grace' and Moments For Moms Volume II and III.

Sabrina feels especially called to the family mountain – women and children, particularly those who have experienced trauma, more specifically domestic & sexual violence. She coaches and mentor youth and young adults that have been victimized and/or experienced trauma in their lives. Being a survivor of such experiences, she easily identifies and empathizes with all who have experienced such. Her faith in and relationship with God has empowered her to be resilient. She is determined to help others experience resurrection power, restoration, and freedom through what she offers in business and ministry. In addition to being an administrator, Sabrina is an educator and advocate that works within her community. She serves on several collaborative teams, taskforces and coalitions. She is the proud wife of Elder Anthony Clemons and the mother of two beautiful, gifted daughters – Rachel and Sarah.

Contact Information

Website: www.sabrinalclemons.com
Email: thekingsagenda12@gmail.com
Facebook: Sabrina Speaks Lyfe

"The same God who sees your strength in motion also honors your stillness."

MOMENTS FOR MOMS

Chapter Five
Dr. Tiffany Sayles
"Running on G"

For years, I lived in a world that spun on the axis of four "Wills"—my husband, Willie, and our three daughters, Willow, Willany, and Willay. It's a line I now say with a laugh, but in the earlier chapters of my life, it was far from funny. Most days, I ran on empty, surviving on fumes, unsure if I'd ever find the strength to breathe deeply again. My reality was one of constant motion, of giving from a well that felt bone dry. But even in those dizzying days, something sacred was taking root: resilience born in the chaos, grace whispered through exhaustion, and the quiet hope that fullness might one day replace the emptiness.

One of the most vivid memories from that season of my life unfolded in my own driveway.

At the time, my husband juggled a full-time job and a full-time catering business, which meant I was often navigating the demands of our household and children on my own. My days began at 4:30 a.m.—the only sliver of time I had to exercise and sit quietly with God before the whirlwind began. From there, the routine was relentless. Wake the girls, get them dressed, fed, and off to school—check. Then came the hour-long commute to my job as a school counselor, where I supported students facing a wide array of challenges, including deep mental health struggles. After a full day of giving, I'd race to pick up the girls, help with homework, listen to their stories, cook, clean, and prepare to do it all again the next day. I can remember wondering constantly—*When do I get to breathe?*

One particular day, chaos peaked. All three girls had afterschool events at different locations and during the same time period. My already small support circle was stretched thin with their own responsibilities, so I found myself doing mental aerobics, trying to be in three places at once. Somehow, I pulled it off. We got through the evening and arrived home late, weary and worn.

On my third trip to unload "all the things" from the car, I noticed the fuel light glowing. My tank was empty—not because I forgot to get gas, but because I didn't have the money for it. And in that moment, something inside me cracked. I sat there in the car, gripping the steering wheel, and cried my heart out. The kind of cry I'm sure the neighbors heard. Inside, my daughters were waiting for their usual prompts to keep them on task with our evening routine. But I couldn't move. I couldn't be the engine that kept everyone running—not this time. All I could do was cry and pray.

I don't remember what I said aloud, but I remember staring at that gas gauge like it was a mirror. I was beyond empty—emotionally, physically, spiritually. I had poured out for everyone: my marriage, my children, my students, my ministry; yet I hadn't left enough to show up for myself. I didn't know the way forward, but deep within, I knew one thing with certainty—something had to change. Life couldn't keep pressing on like this. I cried out to God, confessing that it was all too much, that I was worn thin and didn't know how much longer I could keep going. Then, in the stillness—where time felt suspended—a quiet, steady voice broke through the silence, whispering a truth that anchored me: "My grace is sufficient."

This experience offered me wisdom that I couldn't schedule but also couldn't ignore. In that motionless moment in my driveway, surrounded by exhaustion and silence, I confronted the truth that so many mothers carry but seldom name: giving everything to everyone doesn't mean you're actually okay. It means you've learned to function while empty. I also learned that being needed doesn't equate to being nourished. I had to learn how to be present with myself and tend to the woman behind the many roles. That crying out to God wasn't a sign of weakness but an act of surrender, a turning point from striving and surviving to trusting in something stronger than my own sufficiency.

There was growth in choosing stillness in finally seeing the empty gas tank not as failure but as invitation—an invitation to refill, redefine, and remember myself. Transformation came in realizing that grace doesn't ask you to earn it—it finds you in the driveway, undone, and still calls you enough.

To another mother walking this same tightrope of invisible exhaustion, know that you're not failing—you're just carrying more than anyone sees. But you don't have to carry it alone. It's okay to pause. It's okay to say, "I can't." And it's more than okay to need help. Your value isn't tied to how seamlessly you juggle the chaos. Your worth remains, even on your emptiest day.

I pray that like me, you can look back on this season not with shame, but with a tender kind of reverence—for the woman who kept showing up, even when she felt like she had nothing left to give.

Through that season of exhaustion, when the days blurred together and I felt stretched beyond what I thought possible, my faith quietly anchored me. Not in grand, triumphant moments—but in the whispered prayers, the silent cries behind closed car doors, and the scripture etched into my spirit when words failed me.

It was 2 Corinthians 12:9 that held me together: *"My grace is sufficient for you, for my power is made perfect in weakness."* In a life that demanded strength at every turn, this verse reminded me that I didn't have to navigate this moment, day or season on my own. God wasn't waiting for me to get it all together—He was meeting me below empty with His sufficient grace. I realized grace isn't always soft or serene. Sometimes it shows up in survival mode. In the moment when the gas tank is empty—literally and spiritually—and all you have left is a surrender that sounds a lot like a silent scream.

But even then, grace is still enough.

To any mother walking a similar road, I want to say this:

You are not alone. Your weariness isn't a sign of failure; it's evidence of how deeply you love. But even love needs rest. Give yourself permission to pause. To weep. To be ministered to by silence. God sees your sacrifice, your striving, your unseen prayers whispered over kitchen sinks and car rides. And He's not measuring your worth by how much you carry—but by your willingness to let Him carry you. You don't need to be everything. You just need to be held, filled, and loved.

If you've ever stared at the dashboard of your life and seen the warning light blinking—emotionally, spiritually, or physically—know this: you are not alone, and this isn't the end of your story. Remember-You are allowed to pause. Rest is not a reward—it's a necessity. You don't have to be everything to everyone. You were never meant to carry it all alone. God sees you in the unseen moments. Even when you feel invisible, you are deeply known. His strength is not activated by your perfection, but by your surrender.

A Simple Prayer for Today

Lord, when I feel stretched thin, remind me that I don't have to be strong all the time. Let Your grace fill the cracks where I've run dry. Teach me to rest—not just physically, but in the truth that I am already enough because You are always enough. Even when I'm poured out, I am not forgotten. God's grace fills the spaces where I run empty, and His power rises in the places where I feel weak. Lord please allow Your grace to fill the spaces where I run empty, and Your power to rise in the places where I feel weak. Today, I choose rest, trust, and gentle strength.

A Declaration for Every Day:

Heavenly Father,

You see me when I'm stretched thin and running low. You know the burdens I carry before I can speak them aloud. Today, I come not with perfection, but with a heart in need.

Thank You for the promise in 2 Corinthians 12:9, that Your grace is sufficient for me, and Your power is made perfect in my weakness. When I feel like I have nothing left to give, You are already giving what I need.

Isaiah 40:29 reminds me that You give strength to the weary and increase the power of the weak. So Father, fill these tired hands and this aching heart. Strengthen me not just to survive the day, but to walk in quiet confidence that I am not alone.

Let Psalm 61:2 anchor me—"From the ends of the earth, I cry to You for help when my heart is overwhelmed. Lead me to the rock that is higher than I." When I feel lost in the swirl of responsibilities, lift me to Your steady presence. Be my Rock.

Matthew 11:28-30 whispers to my weary spirit: "Come to Me, all who are weary and burdened, and I will give you rest... for My yoke is easy, and My burden is light." Remind me that I don't have to carry everything—not alone, not ever. Help me trade striving for surrender, and exhaustion for rest in You.

Thank You that Lamentations 3:22-23 still rings true—*"Because of the Lord's great love, we are not consumed, for His compassions never fail.*

They are new every morning; great is Your faithfulness." Even when yesterday drained me, You offer fresh mercy today.

Lord, bless every mother who is quietly pouring herself out, wondering if she's enough. Let her feel Your arms around her, Your strength within her, and Your delight over her. Remind her: She is seen. She is loved and filled by You.

In the name of Jesus, **Amen**.

Refilled by Grace: My
Reflection

Dr. Tiffany Sayles

Dr. Tiffany Sayles is a devoted wife, mother, educator, mentor, and faith-driven leader whose life's work reflects the power of service, resilience, and family. With a doctorate in psychology and a deep commitment to community advocacy, Dr. Sayles has uplifted countless students through initiatives that center emotional wellness and academic excellence. She is known for her compassionate leadership, her dedication to underserved families, and most importantly her unwavering belief in God's purpose which includes serving her family. As a family woman, professional, and spiritual guide, she embodies grace, perseverance, and the values that define faith and family.

Contact Information:

Email: tiffanysayles2024@gmail.com
Facebook: Tiffany Sayles
Instagram: @dr.tsayles

"Surrender doesn't mean giving up; it means trusting God to pick up where you can't."

MOMENTS FOR MOMS

Chapter Six
LaQuana Dena Wigfall
Through the Tears, I Trusted

I thought I had prepared myself for the teenage years—but nothing could have prepared me for the day my son chose his own way over ours.

As a mother, I never imagined the day would come when my child wouldn't want to listen to me—when rebellion would take root in the heart of the boy I raised with so much love. That thought never crossed my mind while he was growing up. But about 3½ years ago, my world changed.

My son was 15½ at the time, and he wanted to have a girlfriend. As his mother, so many thoughts flooded my mind. I still saw him as my baby. But I knew—he was growing up.

He began asking if he could visit her house. Our rule was simple: only if the parents were home. There had to be supervision. At first, everything seemed fine. But over time, he got more serious with this girl. He started to lie. He began staying overnight at her house, even though I was under the impression he was at a friend's. I had even asked the other parents—and they went along with the lie.

When I finally found out—from other people—I was devastated. I couldn't believe my son would deceive me like that.

When you think your child is in one place and they're not, the worry consumes you. Sleepless nights became my normal. I kept wondering, *is someone finally going to be honest with me?* I prayed other adults would help me, not hide the truth, but in reality they wanted to hide the truth from me and something like that will hurt you the most because being left out in the dark when things with your child is going on in one of the worst feelings any mother would ever want to encounter.

One day I gathered the courage to ask him directly. And he denied everything. Or acted like I didn't know what I was talking about. As time went on and he turned 16, things only got worse.
The son I raised no longer seemed like the boy I knew.
He crossed boundaries. He stopped listening to anything I had to say. No matter how hard I tried to reach him, he was closed off.
Then came the day that broke me.

I was in the grocery store—just doing my usual chat when I saw a familiar face. Another mom, someone I knew, walked up and told me something I never expected to hear: *"Your son has been smoking weed with my son. I caught them together."*
My heart shattered. But I didn't let her see my pain. Not in a store full of people. I held it in. I got home, cried, prayed, and eventually broke down.

And then, I let go.
I said, **"Lord, he is Yours. I give him to You."**
It didn't stop there. My son kept going down his path, staying out, smoking, ignoring everything we said. We even took his car away. Nothing worked.

One evening, I felt a panic attack coming on. I prayed to make it home, knowing I could better manage it there. I made it, but as soon as I walked through the door, I collapsed to the floor—crying, begging for help.

My son was home.

I asked him to help me to my bed. But instead of helping his mother, he walked past me—focused on packing his things to move out. He was 16. No one had given him permission, but he was determined.
Thankfully, my aunt came to help. She called the ambulance because I had passed out. At the hospital, they ran tests, checking for any damage. Lying there, overwhelmed and exhausted, I prayed again:
"Lord, please help me. I can't do this alone."

I knew that once he left, he wasn't coming back—not for a while, anyway. But I had peace, because I had already surrendered him to God. Once we surrender Mamas it's up to us to just let God work now. I always said my son was given to me from God, he allowed me to have him for some time but in reality, he is Gods child.

Letting Go, Trusting God

For two years, my son lived with his girlfriend and her family. And for two years, I prayed without ceasing. I asked God for just one thing:
"Let me live to see my son graduate."

And God did just that. I saw him walk across the stage which was one of the happiest days of my life because after all that we went through together God still saw fit for my prayers to be answered and I will forever be grateful for that.

Today, our relationship is so much better. He's not the same boy who walked past me on that floor. And I know—it's all because of God. I trusted Him. I believed it. And He never left my side. Today that same child since then has expressed how sorry he was because he realized that he only has one mother and he never wants me to hurt because of the way he treated me. I forgave my son and I know sometimes Mamas it hurt but we must remember that God forgives us so we must be willing to forgive as well.

Proverbs 22:6
Train up a child in the way he should go: and when he is old, he will not depart from it.

To the Mother Who Feels Alone

Mama, you are not alone.
The same God who held me in my pain will hold you, too. When you've done all, you can, release them into God's care. Pray without ceasing and trust Him to write the ending.

I want to encourage any mother going through what I've been through that you got this don't let anyone tell you that you don't have this because you do have this. Don't be ashamed of what you may be going through or have been through because what's tea to them is your testimony, your story of what you are going or have been through is going to be able to save the next mama who just needs that extra boost of encouragement. God will turn something around if we trust in him that he will do it. I used to think when I was going through that people are going to talk about me, they are going to look at me like I'm the worst mama in the town, it even got to the point where I didn't even want to be seen in the store because I didn't want to be judge from somcone because of what my son and I was going through. But God. But God he turned the mess into me being blessed and today I am thankful for God making me to be a vessel to help another mama that needs to hear my story.

Remember, trouble doesn't last always.
In the midnight hour, God *will* turn things around.

Let this be your prayer:
"Lord, I release my child into Your loving hands. Protect them, guide them, and draw them back to You."

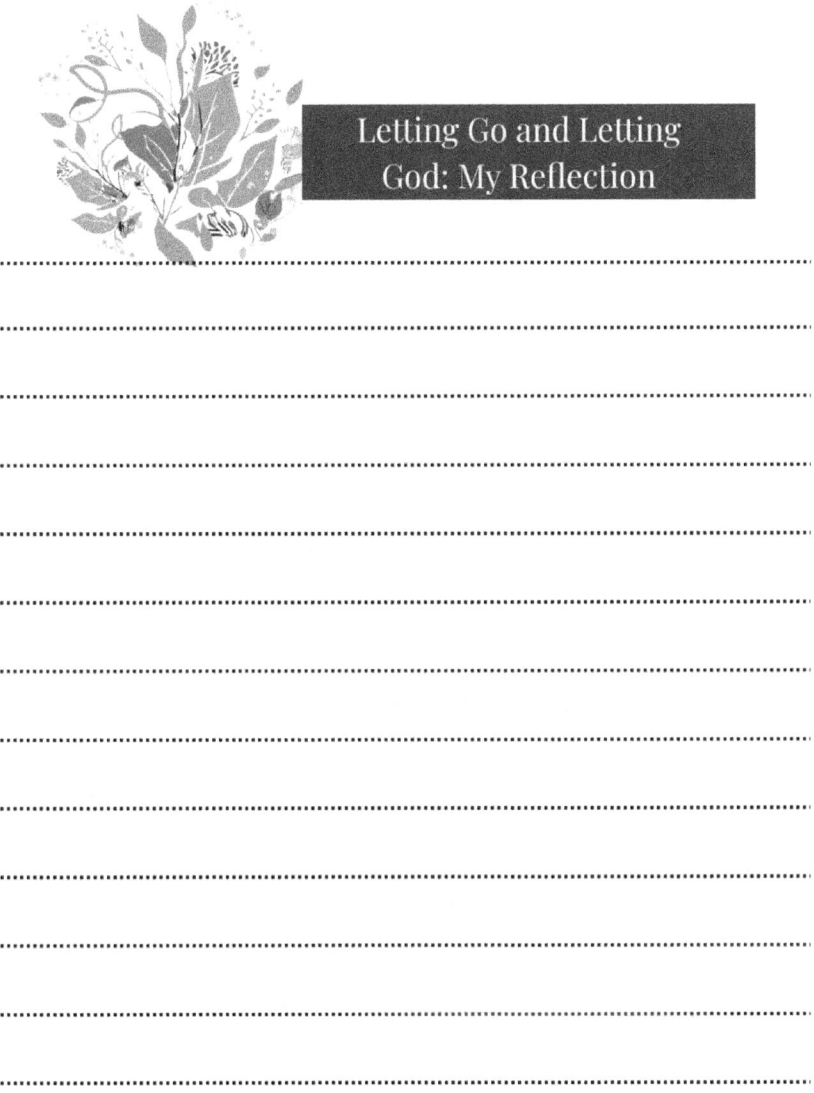

Letting Go and Letting
God: My Reflection

LaQuana Dena Wigfall

LaQuana Wigfall is a wife and mother of three, and a dedicated Family Advocate at an elementary school, committed to supporting families and helping them access essential resources such as food, clothing, housing, and other basic needs. With a strong background in community support, LaQuana is passionate about empowering families to thrive both in and outside of the classroom. She strives to be a dependable source of encouragement and assistance for students and their families, fostering a strong, caring, and connected school community.

Contact Information:

Email: laquanawigfall@gmail.com
Facebook: LaQuana Dena Wigfall

"Grief may bend you, but it cannot break what God has built."

MOMENTS FOR MOMS

Chapter Seven
Dr. Nikki Lawrence
Wisdom and Inspiration Through the Storms

What does a storm look like?

Sometimes it's the wind blowing so violently that everything in its path trembles. Trees bend side to side, unsure if they'll spring back or snap. The sky shifts from light to dark in seconds. Sometimes the rain comes in gentle, almost teasing drops, one at a time—until suddenly it pours.

As a child, storms were simple to me. We turned off all the TVs, lit candles, and stayed close. My grandmother would wrap me in what I called the "suffocating blanket"—heavy, warm, and safe. I would sleep through the thunder because I knew she would be there no matter what the storm brought.

But now, as a woman and mother, storms have changed. They don't always come with thunder or wind. Sometimes they come in silence, wrecking you from the inside out.

The Story of Grief

Over time, my storms started to look different.

My last one was not gentle rain or rolling thunder. It was an unstoppable tornado—private at first, tearing up bones, stealing speech, leaving pain no one could see. Eventually, it could not be hidden. It touched everyone around me.

This storm didn't darken the sky—it lit it up. But the world around me felt dark. Black caskets. Black horses. Black clothes. And there was my grandmother, Granny Louise, lying in stillness.

(Have you ever had to stop and take a breath before you could keep going?)

Have you ever beheld God's beauty in the quiet stillness of someone's homegoing? Have you ever seen the glory of the Lord on a face finally at rest? Have you ever been loved so well by someone, only to watch them step into the reward they've spent a lifetime working toward?

My wisdom, my inspiration, was wrapped in a box. Although she was beautiful, my heart felt selfish. I didn't want to let her go.

Wisdom Gained

Granny Louise was more than my grandmother. She was a provider. An educator. A cook. A prayer warrior. A servant of God. Her life was a living testimony of 1 Corinthians 13:4-7—love that is patient, kind, selfless, and enduring.

She shaped my motherhood in ways I couldn't see until years later.

Her love taught me to reach for my children when they feel alone, just like she reached for me. She reminded me that God is faithful even when life isn't easy.

Her faith kept me grounded. She showed me that parenting comes with both joys and pains—but even the pain can be used by God to heal parts of us we didn't know were broken.

Her service inspired me to give my time and heart to others. I watched her show up for funerals, family reunions, community events—serving without recognition. She taught me that service is not about applause; it's about humility, just as Philippians 2:3-4 reminds us to value others above ourselves.

Her strength showed up in her obedience. She didn't need the glory of man. Even with cancer for much of her life, she walked with God in quiet faith. That's why I gave her flowers every Sunday. I wanted her to enjoy them while she could see them, rather than only when she was gone.

And somewhere in that grief, I learned my own lesson.

I began to read His Word, fast, and pray, and spend time with Him because for the first time I accepted that my mom was not God, and I had to know God for myself. I heard someone say the other day that when they are going through their test, it becomes their testimony, and their testimony will help someone else. That is what I also believe and pray— that as you read my story you are helped, motivated, and encouraged.

Faith & Encouragement

Faith doesn't take the pain away.

But in those moments when my heart felt hollow and my home felt too quiet, God reminded me He was still with me. Psalm 23:4 whispered that even in the valley of the shadow of death, I wasn't walking alone. Revelation 21:4 promised me that one day there will be no more tears, no more mourning, no more pain. Psalm 30:5 reassured me that joy—though delayed—always returns.

I started to see that Granny's legacy wasn't just wisdom—it was faith in action. She didn't just talk about God's promises; she lived like she believed them.

My wisdom didn't just come from Granny Louise. God has placed many women in my life who have shaped me:

- **Jacqueline Wright** taught me to never settle. After losing her husband, she raised two incredible sons with strength and grace she was always a pillar of her community and influence in my life.
- **Michelle Moseley(My Mother)** taught me not to be her but to be better than her—raising four children who , over coming so many obstacles and still coming out on top my Mother just like my Granny is my real hero.
- **My Aunt Bridgette** gave me wisdom to keep my mind strong and my heart humble, to never think I'm better than anyone for wanting more for my family.
- **Deborah A. Smith**—my love's mother—taught me about real love and support. She showed me how to cover my family, cherish them, and protect my peace. She taught me that happiness should be honest and love should be as easy as a laugh.

These women's voices are part of my motherhood toolkit. Their lessons echo in how I love, how I serve, how I pray, and how I lead my home.

Inspiration

My greatest source of wisdom and inspiration will always be my mother. But I also draw strength daily from others:

- **My love, Monte Smith Jr.,** who prays for me and challenges me to be great every day always challenging me to be more and better than the day before.
- **My sisters—Kiki, Sharonda, Shawna, Ebony, Brenda, stacks, Elizabeth and Tayanna**—who hold me accountable. They can pull me aside and tell me when I'm wrong, and I love them for it. They push me to finish what I start.
- **My father,** who taught me to chase education because once you have it, no one can take it away. He also gave me one of my favorite life lessons: that sometimes rain isn't God crying—it's Him inviting you to dance.

These people remind me that storms will always come, but so will God's faithfulness. *Deuteronomy 31:6* reminds me to be strong and courageous because the Lord goes with me and will never leave me. *Philippians 4:13* strengthens me with the truth that I can do all things through Christ. *Jeremiah 29:11* reassures me that His plans are good and full of hope.

Storms change shape. Wisdom sources shift. But God's hand is steady, His promises are sure, and His reward is certain.

Whatever your storm looks like right now—whether it's loud like thunder or silent like grief—know that the same God who walked with my Granny walks with you. He is faithful to comfort, faithful to guide, and faithful to finish the work He's started in you.

Hold His hand. Trust His plan. And let your legacy be one of faith in action.

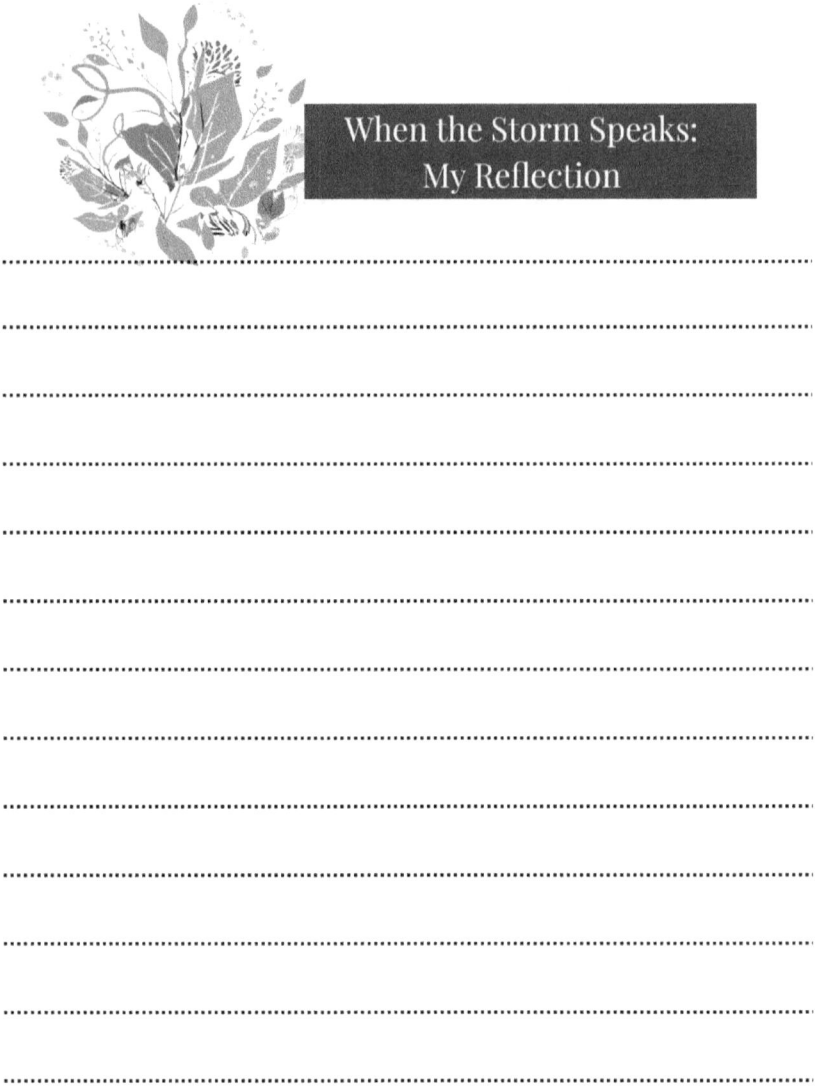

When the Storm Speaks:
My Reflection

Dr. Nikki Lawrence

Dr. Nikki Lawrence, born and raised in Williamsburg, Virginia, is a devoted mother of four (including two bonus children) and the proud partner of Adolph Smith.

Dr. Lawrence has a deep passion for writing, human resources, and serving youth and adults facing mental health challenges. Her work reflects her belief that with **"God and a good glass of tea, anything is possible."**

She is also a returning author, having contributed to *Moments for Moms* Volumes 1 and 2, where she continues to inspire others through her transparency, faith, and heart for helping others heal and grow.

Contact Information:

Email: Drlawc21@gmail.com
Facebook: Nikki Lawrence
Instagram:
@speaksvolumescounselingfirm

"Some of God's greatest miracles happen in the moments no one else sees."

MOMENTS FOR MOMS

Chapter Eight
Crystal D. Harrison M. Ed.
Miracles in the Mundane

"I lift up my eyes to the hills—where does my help come from?
My help comes from the Lord, the Maker of heaven and earth."
—Psalm 121:1–2

I once believed miracles were reserved for rare, unforgettable experiences—the kind that leave you breathless, in awe, and with a story worth retelling. But motherhood reshaped that belief. It taught me that some of the greatest miracles don't shout; they whisper. They happen in the quiet, repetitive, often unseen rhythms of ordinary life.

A Mother's Chaos

In the early years, my world was filled with the chaos only mothers of little ones can truly understand. I had three children under four, and life felt like a blur of sticky fingers, sleepless nights, and Cheerios scattered in unexpected places. Every day carried both the weight of exhaustion and the wonder of raising little lives who needed me for everything.

One morning, I was already drained before the day had even officially begun. Jessika had cried through the night with teething pain. Juanita had discovered the thrill of pulling everything out of the cabinets, leaving pots, pans, and cereal boxes all over the floor. And J.T. had decided clothes were unnecessary, which meant chasing him down with tiny socks and shirts while he squealed with laughter, determined to win the game.

By nine o'clock, we had already endured three meltdowns, a diaper blowout that left me scrubbing the carpet, and a cup of orange juice that somehow managed to splatter across the counter and drip from the ceiling. The mess around me looked like evidence of failure, and my heart echoed the same.

I collapsed on the couch, tears threatening to spill, whispering to myself: Is this really what I was made for? Am I even a good mother?

God's Gentle Reminder

That afternoon, as I sat folding laundry, J.T. walked over with his little Ninja Turtle clutched in his hand. He looked at me with innocent sincerity and said, "Mommy, you're doing such a good job."

I froze. His words pierced through the fog of fatigue and doubt. To me, nothing felt "good enough." But to him, I was more than enough. God used the innocent voice of my child to remind me that this season wasn't about perfection—it was about presence.

That evening, as I rocked Juanita to sleep, humming softly "Open the Eyes of My Heart, Lord," I felt peace settle over me. The laundry still buzzed in the dryer, the dishes still waited in the sink, and the floor was still sticky—but in the middle of it all, God was there.

The Sacred in the Ordinary

Motherhood taught me that miracles are not always found in milestones. Sometimes, they are hidden in faithfulness—showing up again and again, even when it feels like too much.

I remember when J.T. was around five or six years old, and we had one of those terrifying "emergency room" days. He had been playing outside with a friend, running fast and free the way children do, when he tripped on the rocks. The fall left him with a cut just above his left eye, and the blood seemed to come from everywhere at once.

My heart raced, my hands shook, and for a split second I thought, I can't do this. Yet somehow, God steadied me. I scooped him up, whispering prayers as I rushed to the car. At the hospital, I held his hand tightly as the doctors worked to stitch the wound. His tears flowed, and I wiped them away while trying to smile through my own. I wanted him to see bravery on my face even though fear pounded in my chest.

Not long after, another accident happened—this time a broken arm. J.T. had been playing a game on the bleachers with a friend, sliding across and trying to push each other off. What began as innocent fun ended with a hard fall and a loud crack. I can still remember the way he cried out, clutching his arm, and how helpless I felt in that moment when his father carried him inside from the basketball court.

Once again, we sat in a waiting room. Once again, I felt the familiar mix of fear, helplessness, and fierce love. And once again, I realized something powerful: even here—in the chaos, the pain, the unexpected interruptions—God's presence was near.

Looking back, those moments were just as holy as bedtime prayers and nursery rhymes. The stitches and broken bones reminded me that motherhood is not about creating a picture-perfect life. It's about walking with your children through every valley, trusting God to be present in the details, and allowing His strength to carry you when yours runs out.

A Shift in Faith

The truth is, God was shaping me through the very moments that felt like they were undoing me. My patience grew—not because I had mastered motherhood, but because I kept showing up. My love deepened—not because I had all the answers, but because God's love carried me through.

Before motherhood, I thought faith was about doing big things for God. But as the years went on, I realized faith is also about needing Him in every breath, every moment, every seemingly ordinary task.

Psalm 121:1–2 became my anchor: *"I lift up my eyes to the hills—where does my help come from? My help comes from the Lord, the Maker of heaven and earth."*

I began to lift my eyes not just in moments of triumph but in the ordinary—and even the frightening. And every time, He was there.

Encouragement for the Weary Mother

To the mama who feels overlooked, overwhelmed, or underqualified: you are not invisible. God sees you. He delights in your faithfulness.

He sees the scraped knees you bandage, the late-night prayers you whisper, the quiet courage it takes to walk into another doctor's office. He is not measuring your worth by how well you hold it all together. He is holding you.

Here's a practice that helped me: pause in the middle of the mess, take a deep breath, and whisper, "Jesus, help me."

I even left myself reminders. On my fridge, a sticky note read: "You are doing holy work." Because sometimes the ordinary doesn't feel holy, but in God's hands—it always is.

Reflection

Take a few minutes to pause and reflect:

1. **Where have you seen God's presence in your ordinary day?**
   Was it in a kind word, a moment of peace, or even in the middle of chaos?

2. **What part of your motherhood feels the most mundane or difficult right now?**
   Write it down. Ask God to reveal how He is at work in that very place.

3. **How do you define faithfulness in this season?**
   Where are you showing up day after day that deserves more recognition than you've given yourself?

4. **Read Psalm 121:1–2 again.**
   What does it stir in your heart? How can you "lift your eyes" more often throughout your daily routines?

5. **Choose one way to connect with God today.**

   o   A sticky note of scripture

   o   A prayer whispered in the kitchen

   o   A worship song while folding laundry

Father,

Thank You, for meeting me in the middle of what feels ordinary and even overwhelming. Thank You for being with me in the scraped knees, the stitches, the broken arms, and the midnight tears. Help me see that these moments matter to You. Give me strength to keep showing up, even when I feel weak, and remind me that nothing is wasted in Your hands. Thank You for grace for today and hope for tomorrow.

Amen.

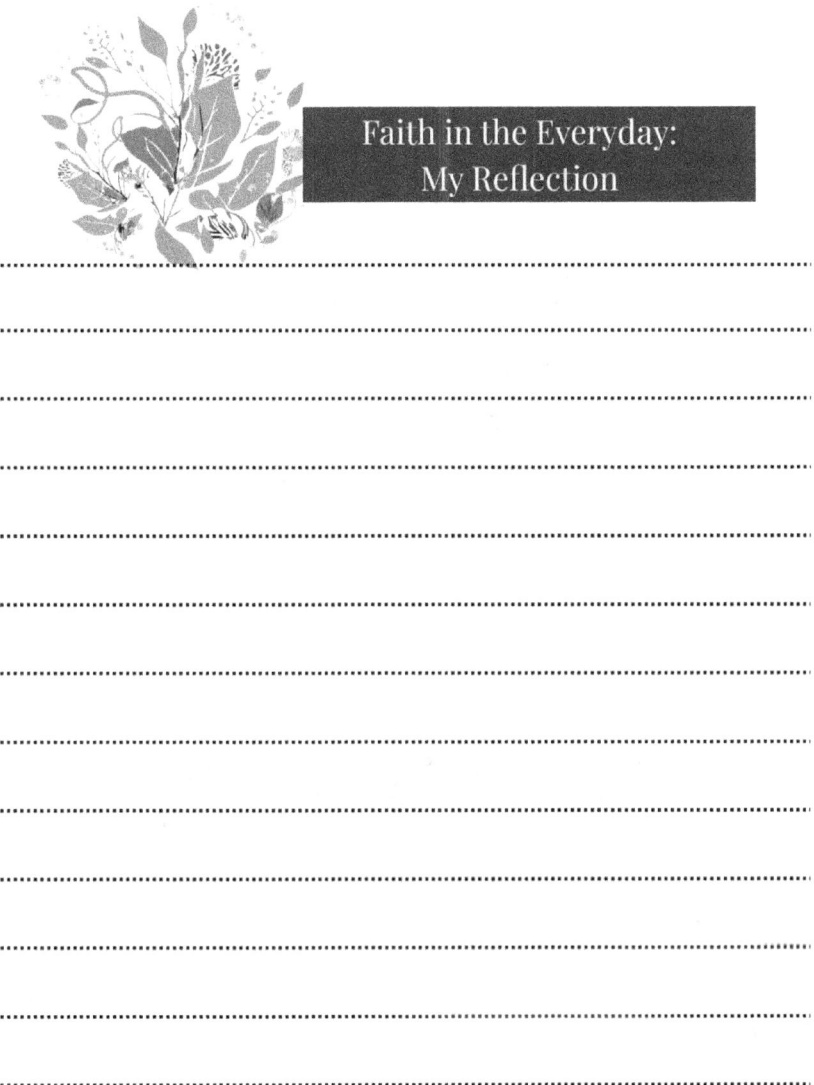

Faith in the Everyday:
My Reflection

Crystal D. Harrison M. Ed.

Crystal Denise Harrison is truly a woman after God's own heart. She strives to "Raise the Standards" one opportunity, one woman, and one purpose at a time as she guides others to discover their purpose and destiny in the Father.

Crystal resides in Chester, Pennsylvania, with her husband Jay of thirty-eight years. Together, they are the proud parents of seven children—two of whom have passed away, "the Twinz"—and the loving grandparents of eight.

A graduate of Hampton University, Crystal earned her Bachelor's degree in Liberal Arts with a concentration in Early Childhood Education, later completing her Master's degree in Early Childhood Education at the University of Phoenix. With over thirty years in the ECE field, she continues to provide training, mentorship, and resources to other professionals and childcare organizations through her work with Circle of Educators and CDH ECE Educational Resources and Services.

Crystal is the founder of **CDH Ministries** and **Heart 2 Heart**, a mentoring and fellowship program designed to restore the hearts of women and help them experience the fullness of God's love and purpose. Her compassion and commitment to serving others are the foundation of her mission to help women heal and thrive.

She is the author of *How to Fight Fair in Marriage*, *The Traits of Women of Grace*, and *Thirty Days of Prayer for Foster Parents & Adoptive Families*. In addition, she has contributed to *Moments for Moms Volumes 2 & 3* and *Faith While Waiting*, and is the author of the children's book *A Bug's Life Alphabet Book*.

Contact Information:

Email: 4cdhministries@gmail.com
Website: www.CDHMinistries.com
Facebook: Crystal Denise Harrison
Heart 2 Heart
Circle of Educators
Instagram: @cdhministries

"Forgiveness
doesn't erase
what happened—
it breaks the
chain that keeps
you bound to it."

MOMENTS FOR MOMS

Chapter Nine
Cheryl Lynne
The Cry Behind My Prayer

Before I ever gave birth, I knew the kind of parent I wanted to be—one who protected, nurtured, prayed, and most of all, broke the cycle. When you're carrying a child, your mind shifts. You make promises to this little life inside of you—to protect, love, and support them. You vow that they will never experience the loneliness, rejection, and hurt that you did.

So, you pray. You pray that your child will never face what you faced. And as they grow, you do your best to teach, love, and protect them.

As a young mother, I was protective. I kept my child close and only trusted family to watch them—because I believed family wouldn't cause harm. I was intentional, cautious, and prayerful. I taught my child about good touch and bad touch. I crossed every "t" and dotted every "i."

Years passed—about twelve. I had grown into a more seasoned, patient parent. I thought I had done everything right.

Then, on a cold winter day, everything changed.

I was standing in my kitchen, sipping hot chai tea, when my phone rang. It was my child, now a young adult, calling from overseas. The first thirty minutes were full of laughter and warm memories. Then, their voice cracked.

"Mom," they said softly, "I need to talk to you about something."

Time slowed. Suddenly, my memory box opened—age two, five, eight—every stage of their life flashed through my mind. I tried to stay present, but my heart began to ache.

Then came the words no parent ever wants to hear: someone had touched them inappropriately.

I couldn't breathe. Questions rushed through my mind. *Who? When? Where?* I replayed every moment, every face, every memory. Then, the bomb dropped—it was someone from within our own family.

I had let the monster into my home.

That night, I couldn't sleep. My mind replayed every word my child said. I was angry, confused, heartbroken, and full of guilt. In that season, I was still young in my faith. I cried out to God, "Why? Why my child?"

I had prayed for protection. I thought I had done everything right. Yet, here I was, living my worst fear.

I questioned everything—my parenting, my prayers, even my purpose. I wondered if God had heard me at all.

The pain was unimaginable. As parents, we do all we can to protect our children, but sometimes the danger comes from the very place we thought was safest.

My child needed protection—and I couldn't protect her. What hurt even more was learning that she held it in for so long. She told me she didn't think I could speak up for her because of my speech impediment. That broke me.

As she shared her story, I had to do something no parent is ever prepared for—sit in the pain, listen, and be still. I had to set aside my guilt, my rage, and my heartbreak to focus on her healing.

Yes, the wounds were fresh. Yes, I wanted justice. But it wasn't about me—it was about her.

When your child is hurting, your pain takes a back seat. I held back my tears while she spoke, but later that night, I broke down. I cried until I couldn't cry anymore. I screamed, hollered, and asked God why He didn't stop it. I blamed myself.

For months, my child and I struggled to rebuild our relationship. There were moments of anger, confusion, and silence. I realized that my child was doing the work to heal, but I wasn't. I felt stuck—like quicksand pulling me back into the same darkness I once escaped as a child.

Then one rainy night, I hit a breaking point. Crying uncontrollably, I heard a gentle voice say, *"Breathe, forgive, and give grace."*

I kept asking, *"Why?"*

And the voice replied, *"Because I did the same for you."*

Scriptures began to come to me—
Mark 11:25: *"Whenever you stand praying, forgive, if you have*

anything against anyone, so that your Father also who is in heaven may forgive you your trespasses."
Matthew 5:22: *"Everyone who is angry with his brother will be liable to judgment."*

I knew it was the Holy Spirit speaking to me. That conviction stayed with me for weeks. Eventually, I sat down and had difficult conversations with everyone involved. Some were open; others weren't. Through prayer, I learned to listen—to be still—and to forgive.

I had to forgive myself first. I had to release the guilt, shame, and anger I carried. Forgiveness didn't mean forgetting—it meant freeing myself from bondage.

In that season, God taught me what true forgiveness looks like. He showed me that letting go doesn't make you weak—it allows healing to begin. I learned to build healthy boundaries, love from a distance, and accept that not everyone is ready to heal.

And that's okay.

My job now is to guide, comfort, support, and pour love into my children. I refuse to let the next generation repeat what we went through.

Prayer became my anchor. I realized I had been praying, but not effectively—praying out of fear instead of faith. God taught me how to pray with purpose.

Prayer for Forgiveness and Family Protection

Heavenly Father,
Please help me step outside of my pain and emotions. Give me strength to forgive others as You have forgiven me. Remind me that people need grace, because none of us are perfect.

Your Word says in Proverbs 10:12, "Hatred stirs up strife, but love covers all offenses."
So today and always, I choose love.

Teach me the right words to say when facing those who have hurt me. Let my response be filled with grace, not bitterness. Help me forgive even when there's no apology or acknowledgment.

I declare that no weapon formed against my family shall prosper. Surround us with Your angels wherever we go. I rebuke every attack— spiritual or physical—that tries to come against us.

Lord, You loaned my children to me, so I return them to You. I refuse to carry the burden of fear any longer. My family is blessed and highly favored.

They will walk in purpose, excel in all they do, and fulfill every plan You have for their lives.

In Jesus' name,
Amen.

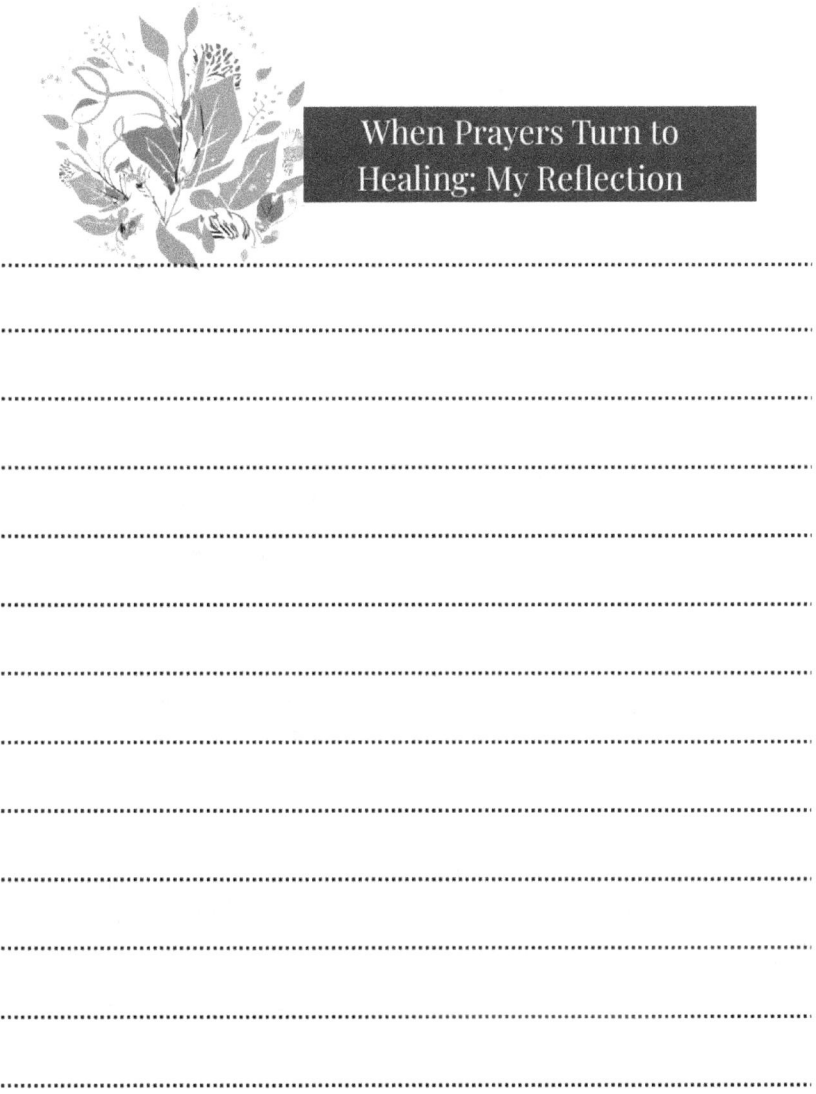

When Prayers Turn to
Healing: My Reflection

Cheryl Lynne

Cheryl Lynne is a dedicated Family Advocate Partner serving Philadelphia and Delaware, bringing over 16 years of experience in family advocacy and more than a decade of training in mental health. Her expertise includes DBT (Dialectical Behavior Therapy) skills and trauma-informed care.

Cheryl is passionate about empowering families to find and use their voices—encouraging storytelling as a powerful tool for connection and healing. She currently serves on several boards, including the Philadelphia System of Care (CBH), Philadelphia Family Voices, the

Historic Overlook Colony in Delaware, and the 7th RD District Delaware Democratic State Committee.

Beyond her advocacy work, Cheryl is the founder of **Embrace with Wuv**, an organization that mentors young ladies ages 8 to 24. Through workshops on self-esteem, leadership, and empowerment—including her signature one-day conference *Ladies to Queens*—she helps young women embrace themselves with confidence and purpose, particularly during life transitions such as their menstrual journey.

Cheryl's mission is to equip families and young women with the tools, understanding, and confidence to use their voices and stories as pathways to empowerment and change.

Contact Information:

Facebook: Cheryl Miller
IG: @embracewithwuvl.l.c
www.cherylscorner.com

"*God doesn't ask you to have it all together; He just asks you to keep coming to Him.*"

MOMENTS FOR MOMS

Chapter Ten
Stephanie Wills
The Strength I Didn't Know I Had

Have you ever felt like the weight of the world was on your shoulders, and the only thing you could do was whisper, "God help me"?

There was a quiet morning, when I found myself standing in the kitchen, clutching a coffee mug and whispering the only words I had left: "God help me." That prayer wasn't long or eloquent – it was raw desperate, and holy. It set the tone for a season that would challenge me more deeply than I ever imagined.

Motherhood has a way of unearthing the parts of us we never knew needed healing. Psalms 46:1 says, *"God is our refuge and strength, an ever-present help in trouble."* That verse anchored me then- and it still does now. My youngest had just turned two, and my oldest was navigating the rocky world of middle school. I was in the thick of early childhood chaos, with the added emotional weight of watching one child inch closer to adolescence.

That day, everything came crashing down when both kids were sick, the laundry was piling up, and I felt completely unseen. I remember sitting on the bathroom floor, crying quietly so they wouldn't hear me. I felt I had failed as a mom, as a woman of faith. I felt overwhelmed, inadequate, exhausted and deep lonely. I wanted to be strong for everyone, but I didn't know where to draw strength from.

It was in that low moment I whispered the prayer that changed everything, not because God removed my circumstances immediately, but because He met me in the mess. I began noticing small moments of grace: a kind word, a nap that actually lasted, a moment of laughter with my kids. Those small glimpses of light reminded me that God was near, even in my exhaustion.

That experience taught me that strength doesn't always look like having it all together. Sometimes, real strength is found in surrender. I learned that prayer isn't just a spiritual discipline- it's a lifeline, especially in motherhood. Through that hard season, I experienced spiritual transformation. I now understand the beauty of dependence on God and how He shows up even in the most mundane moments of motherhood.

The lesson? You don't have to carry it all, because He already is.

In the middle of my overwhelm, it was my faith that anchored me. I didn't always have the words to pray, but I had the presence of God. He met me where I was- not in perfection, but in persistence. One verse that deeply encouraged me during this time was Isaiah 41:10: *"Do not fear, for I am with you; do not be dismayed, for I am your God. I will strengthen you and help you; I will uphold you with my righteous right hand."* I clung to that promise like a lifejacket.

Through every messy moment, God gently reminded me that I was never alone. My faith didn't remove the hard days, but it gave me the courage to walkthrough them. If you're in a similar season, feeling unseen, unheard, or uncertain, I want to tell you this: God sees you. He hears your whispered prayers and catches every tear. You are not forgotten. Let these words be your reminder: You are doing sacred work. Even when the laundry is never-ending and the emotional load feels too heavy, God is with you- guiding, sustaining, and equipping you with grace for each day.

When you feel unseen, remember this: God sees every act of love, service, and sacrifice you offer your family. Take a moment today and breathe deeply. Write down three ways God has shown up for you this week- even in small ways.

Speak this truth over yourself:

"I am called, I am capable, and I am covered by God's grace."

Keep this close when days feel long. You are not just surviving, you are sowing seeds of love that will bloom in time.

*Thank you, Lord for walking with me in every season of motherhood. When I feel weak, remind me that your strength is made perfect in my weakness. Help me to mother with grace, love with intention, and trust you daily. May I see your hand in both the chaos and the quiet, and rest in the truth I am never alone. **Amen.***

Grace for the Weary: My
Reflection

Stephanie Wills

Stephanie Wills was born in 1962, the fifth child of five to Mr. and Mrs. Weldon Johnson. Stephanie's passion for writing started at the age of five where she wrote many fantasy stories as a child. In her spare time she enjoys taking care of her children, swimming, bowling, and traveling.

As years went by, her dream and vision of owning a daycare center became a reality. She has been up and operating now for forty-four years. This was just one. Of the many great accomplishments that she has achieved. As Stephanie continues with her passion for writing she has now completed four inspirational books, Phases of life, The Road to Emotional Healing, and Flowing Waters Presents: Poems of the Nile (First and Second Edition) and her most recent release, I'm Addicted to My Children. She currently resides in Philadelphia, PA.

Contact Information:

Email: willsstr@aol.com
Facebook: Stephanie Wills

"God's plans don't expire with age — they unfold with purpose."

MOMENTS FOR MOMS

Chapter Eleven
Lillian Jackson
The Second Time Around

And it came to pass... the prayer I prayed over 20 years ago really happened — at 44 years old.

I started sleeping a lot, I didn't think much of it. I wasn't thinking I was pregnant — honestly, I thought I was just bloated. One time at work, my supervisor asked me, "Are you pregnant?" because of the cravings I was having. I wanted watermelon and corn on the cob. I looked at her like she was crazy: "Girl, I'm 44! No, I'm not pregnant!"

But that Monday, I was working with one of my patients who had impaired speech and didn't talk much. As I bent down to hug him, his eyes got big. He said, "Who pregnant?" But he meant *you* pregnant. I froze. I had to make sure that's what he said. That was my second sign about my son.

Still, I stayed in denial. I didn't go to the doctor.

Then came the third sign.

While at a family cookout, my nephew hugged me. Instead of coming to me, he went straight to my son's father and said, "Her stomach felt hard." His dad came to me and said, "Maybe you should go get checked out."

I was defensive. "Checked out for what?"

He said, "Because when your nephew hugged you, he noticed your belly felt hard. You might want to take a pregnancy test."

So I went to the store and got one. Took the test. And it was **positive**.

The anxiety hit me so hard before I even saw the results. I was standing at a crossroads in my life. I was scared. *How am I going to take care of a baby?* I haven't done this in 22 years!

His father and I weren't even in a good place mentally, spiritually, or financially. I was completely overwhelmed.

I finally went to the doctor, and they told me I was already five months pregnant. I almost passed out. That news shook my whole world. I needed help — and honestly, I still do.

After finding out, I started smoking cigarettes even more. I was stressed, worried, and scared. His father was deep in drug addiction, and I was trying so hard to hold everything together. I worked the entire pregnancy — all nine months, right up until the day I went into the hospital. I was emotionally drained and just trying to survive.

But I talked to God. I said, "Lord, I can't do this. You have to help me. I don't want this baby to die, and I don't want to die either."

That prayer came from my soul.

Then I ended up in the hospital — my asthma had flared up so bad. I was there for a whole week. They gave me every treatment they could. When they finally released me, I was on a bag full of medications.

But I never picked up another cigarette again.

That Friday, I finished my shift. That night, I was back in the hospital. They induced labor and tried everything. But I barely dilated — three to four centimeters after all those hours. Then I caught an infection. They started me on antibiotics fast. Eventually, they had to do an emergency C-section.

My anxiety was through the roof.

But God showed up.

I had a beautiful, healthy baby boy — 8 pounds, 15 ounces, 19½ inches long. We smiled. His father was there for the birth. He left afterwards and said he'd be back... but I didn't see him again until I made it home.

One of my sisters had to be my support. She came, picked me and Baby Z up, and helped get us home.

Writing this brings tears to my eyes.

We went through **so much**. His dad's addiction, fear, stress. But **God carried us**. We kept it pushing.

This second time around was nothing like the first.

My daughter — my baby girl, now a grown woman — was easy. She was my joy. My ride or die. I had her during my wild years — doing drugs, out partying, fighting, chasing men. And even as a little girl in diapers, she would wipe my tears and say, "Mommy, don't cry."

Even with all my mess, God protected her. She's now working on her third degree, already holding her Bachelor's in Political Science, her Master's in Public Administration, and now she's working on her PhD in Education — hoping to graduate in 2027.

She still walks with Christ. She still represents Him. I raised her in the Word — even when I was in the streets, God never left her. This is a baby that supported me as a baby, wiping my tears and still supports me now. Just to think, I almost aborted this baby girl. I praise God that it didn't happen that way.

People said that I wasn't going to make it, not after all the sexual abuse and trauma I faced from childhood into adulthood. But God!

I thank and praise God I'm here to tell the story.

I'd be lying if I said it wasn't hard.

I really thought it would be easier this time. I'd been drug-free for 24 years. I'd rededicated my life to Christ. I just thought things would be smoother. But when my son was six years old, he was diagnosed as moderately on the autism spectrum. I didn't want to accept it. I cried... but God is helping me to understand and grow. He is helping me raise this child.

He is **still** helping me.

There were nights I would pack my baby up and go out looking for his father at two and three o'clock in the morning. I did it so much, my son thought it was normal. One day, I had to sit him down and say, "No baby, this isn't normal. I did it because I love you and I wanted our family to work."

But I finally had to let go after being in the relationship for 24 years. Oh my goodness, this was so hard for me to do.

2 Timothy 4:7 says (GNT):
"I have done my best in the race. I have run the full distance, and I have kept the faith."

I fought hard for my children. I fought hard for our family. But now I've put the gloves down. I surrender. I let God fight for me.

Like Donnie McClurkin says, "After you've done all you can... just stand." That's from Ephesians 6 — and it's the truth.

And I hold on to Jeremiah 29:11:
"For I know the plans I have for you, declares the Lord... plans to prosper you and not to harm you..."

That scripture still comforts me. As moms, sometimes we feel like the weight of the world is on our shoulders. But God's plan is never to harm us — it's always to help us.

That's peace. That was peace then. And it still is now.

When Life Catches You Off Guard

1. How Do I Respond When Life Disrupts My Plans?
● Do I panic, numb out, or push through?
● What emotions am I carrying right now that I haven't named or faced?

> *"Trust in the Lord with all your heart and lean not on your own understanding." – Proverbs 3:5*

2. How Has God Been Faithful Before — and Can I Trust Him Again?
● When has God made a way for me in the past?
● Can I choose to remember His goodness even in uncertainty?

> *"I will remember the deeds of the Lord... Yes, I will remember your miracles of long ago." – Psalm 77:11*

3. What Part of My Story Might Be Healing for Someone Else?
● Am I willing to be honest about my struggles and victories?
● Who might need to hear my testimony?

> *"They overcame him by the blood of the Lamb and the word of their testimony." – Revelation 12:11*

4. Where Is the Beauty in My Broken Places?
● What has this unexpected season revealed about my strength, my faith, or my purpose?
● How can I honor what I've survived?

"He gives beauty for ashes, the oil of joy for mourning..." –
Isaiah 61:3

5. Am I Willing to Let Go, Trust God, and Just Stand?

• What does "just standing" look like for me today?
• Can I believe that God's plan is not to harm me — but to prosper me?
"After you've done all you can... just stand." – *Ephesians 6:13*
"For I know the plans I have for you..." – *Jeremiah 29:11*

When God Rewrites the
Story: My Reflection

Lillian Jackson

Lillian I. Jackson is a devoted woman of God with a true heart for serving others. A lifelong resident of Chester, Pennsylvania, she was educated in the Chester Upland School District and continues to give back to her community through faith and service.

She faithfully serves at Anointed Full Gospel Methodist church where she is a member. She works closely with her Overseer in the Merge Ministry and contributes to several other ministries. In addition to her church involvement, Lillian has a strong background in nursing. She is a full-time hospice aide and also works overnight in skilled nursing, caring for those in need with compassion and dedication.

Lillian is the proud mother of two wonderful children—her 30-year-old daughter and her 8-year-old son—who inspire her daily. Currently, she is pursuing biblical studies through the Alliance of Eagle Institute to deepen her knowledge of God's Word. With a continual thirst for righteousness, Lillian strives to walk faithfully in her journey of life, service, and ministry.

Contact Information:

Email: lillyijackson42@gmail.com
TikTok- @lil57629
Instagram- lilimfavoredjackson
Facebook- Lillian Jackson

"Faith doesn't make the mountain smaller — it gives you the strength to climb."

MOMENTS FOR MOMS

Chapter Twelve
Valencia Franklin
I Won't Give Up

"We plan, but the Lord orders our steps." — **Proverbs 16:9**

We can set goals, dream as big as the sky, and fill our days with plans, but if those plans don't align with what God has for us, the road to get there will be harder. God is always in control.

I've learned to want my plans to line up with the destiny and purpose God has for me. I put my trust in Him because I know He is my keeper— and He keeps His promises.

Continuing to trust God's plan is an everyday decision. I choose God.

When we stop trying to control the narrative of our lives and allow God to be God, we'll begin to see just how great the steps He orders truly are.

Where does my story begin?

Teen mom. Grew up in poverty. Experienced abuse. The struggle was real, y'all.

I got pregnant at sixteen. A trip to the clinic and Planned Parenthood were in my near future, but God had other plans. I gave birth to my daughter shortly after my seventeenth birthday, and my life changed forever.

I had to grow up fast—get a job, take night classes, and work hard to graduate high school. I missed out on so many fun moments as a teenager, **but God!**

By the time I reached my twenties, I was raising four children. Then came a day I'll never forget—**November 29, 2015.**My second child, my sweet Madalyn, was diagnosed with stage four cancer.

What we thought would be a routine surgery to remove lymph nodes turned into a diagnosis that shook our world. She was only four years old. Madalyn fought courageously for five years. She was the strongest little person I've ever known. Her journey touched countless lives all across the country.

A highlight of her story was meeting actor **Chadwick Boseman**, who played Black Panther and many other iconic roles. Maddy's photo with him was even featured in *People* magazine.

She passed away in 2021 at just nine years old. Though she is gone, her impact remains deeply rooted in the hearts of so many.

Let me catch you up to where I am now—I'm a single mother of five beautiful children. While Maddy was battling cancer, I was in nursing school and working two jobs: as a manager at McDonald's and on the overnight shift at Amazon.

Through God's grace, I graduated from nursing school in 2023 with my associate's degree and became a Registered Nurse. I now work full-time at a local hospital and sometimes supervise at nursing homes. But my personal favorite role? Mentoring others. I started my own business tutoring nursing students, and it has become so much more than tutoring. It's ministry. It's mentoring. It's purpose.

There's no greater feeling than seeing someone succeed and knowing you played a part in their journey.

I also founded **Maddy's Miracle Foundation**, a nonprofit dedicated to giving back to the community and helping families affected by cancer. It's my way of keeping Madalyn's legacy alive while honoring the strength and love she showed the world.

Everything I've been through—every trial, every victory—has made me the woman I am today.

Some experiences were good, others painful, but through them all, I learned.

I learned that storms don't last forever. Eventually, the rain stops, and the rainbow appears.

People come into your life for a season and a reason. Some will be blessings, others will be lessons—but you'll know which is which by the fruit they bear and the mark they leave on your life.

If I could offer advice to another mother walking a similar path, it would be this:

Keep God first. Surround yourself with positive people—those who encourage you, believe in you, and remind you of your worth. They don't have to share your exact goals, but they should share your faith and mindset.

The road is not meant to be easy, but God places people along the way to help you keep moving forward.

Don't give up. Don't stop.

Faith means complete trust or confidence in someone or something. For me, that "someone" is God.

My faith has kept me whole, healthy, and sane. It's what allowed me to survive loss, raise my children, and chase my dreams.

Prayer keeps me grounded. I spend time in my prayer closet, journaling, reflecting, and sitting in quiet moments with God. I find strength through my church family, Bible studies, and women's groups.

My faith shows up in every area of my life.

No matter what I face, I trust that God will make a way. He keeps me covered and safe.

"But those who hope in the Lord will renew their strength.
They will soar on wings like eagles;
they will run and not grow weary,
they will walk and not be faint." — **Isaiah 40:31**

Just because you can't see how the story ends doesn't mean you should give up.

The prophet **Habakkuk** wrote:

"For still the vision awaits its appointed time;
it hastens to the end—it will not lie.
If it seems slow, wait for it;
it will surely come; it will not delay." — **Habakkuk 2:2–3**

There will come a day when your tears fall—not because of your troubles, but because God has answered your prayers.

Hold on. Trust His timing. Keep the faith.

Because with God—**you will not give up, and you will not lose.**

Unshakeable Hope: My Reflection

Valencia Franklin

Valencia Franklin is a dedicated mother, Registered Nurse, and contributing writer for Moments for Moms: Legacy Unlocked Magazine. A single mother of five, Valencia's journey is one of perseverance, faith, and purpose. She became a mother as a teenager and went on to pursue her nursing degree at Bishop State Community College in Mobile, Alabama—all while caring for her daughter, Maddy, who bravely battled cancer for five years.

Though Maddy passed away at the age of nine, her legacy continues through Maddy's Miracle, the nonprofit Valencia founded in her honor. The organization provides $500 scholarships to high school seniors who have faced hardship, encouraging them to keep moving forward despite life's challenges.

Valencia now works as a Registered Nurse and runs a tutoring business supporting nursing students as they pursue their dreams. Her story is a testament to resilience and faith—reminding others that even in moments of weakness, God's strength prevails.

Her message to mothers everywhere: Keep your faith, make time for yourself, and never forget that God chose you for the title of "Mom" for a reason.

Contact Information:

Email: valenciaim23@gmail.com
Facebook: Valencia Franklin

"God met me in the cracks of my story and made something beautiful out of what was broken."

MOMENTS FOR MOMS

Chapter Thirteen
Devon Garrison
Faith Beyond Beauty

I used to think beauty was found in the picture-perfect moments — the smiles, the milestones, the carefully curated memories. But motherhood taught me that true beauty is often hidden in the messy, unfiltered moments — the ones that bring you to your knees. There were days when I felt completely undone, unsure if I had what it took to be the mother my children needed. It was in those moments that faith became more than a word; it became my anchor.

Have you ever looked at your life and wondered if the cracks and broken pieces could ever be made whole again? I did. And yet, in those very cracks, God showed me something greater than my pain. He showed me that faith could carry me beyond what I could see — beyond fear, beyond doubt, beyond the picture-perfect life I thought I needed — to something far more beautiful.

A Season of Trials

The season that taught me the most about faith came during the late years of motherhood. I can still remember the constant cycle of sleepless nights, endless cries, and the thought of not seeing my baby again. My body was exhausted, my emotions were frayed, and my mind was filled with quiet questions I was almost afraid to say out loud:

Is this really happening? How did this happen? It's my fault I should have stayed.

Yet, I also felt that staying could make things worse.

One night stands out vividly. It was approximately 6 p.m., and I pulled up to the house he was staying at, only to be told that he was not there and no one knew when he would return. Standing in the freezing cold from 6–10 p.m., tears streamed down my face. I felt completely empty — physically, emotionally, and spiritually. In that moment, I prayed the simplest prayer I had ever prayed:

"God, I can't do this without You."

That prayer didn't fix everything instantly, but it opened my heart in a new way.

Faith in the Breaking

Slowly, I began to notice the small ways God was meeting me right where I was. A peace like never before filled my heart. I started to worship with the song "A Mighty Long Way, Lord," and He reminded me:

"This is only temporary, not permanent."

Faith became the thread that held me together when everything else felt like it was unraveling.

The turning point came when I realized that motherhood wasn't asking me to be perfect — it was inviting me to be present, even in the messy moments. I stopped trying to make everything look beautiful and started looking for the beauty that was already there: remembering I had another child who needed me, noticing the small victories of each day. Faith didn't take away the hard parts, but it gave me the courage to keep showing up with love, even when I felt broken.

Looking back, that season taught me that beauty isn't always polished or Instagram-worthy. Sometimes beauty is raw, unfiltered, and wrapped in the quiet strength that only faith can give. That's what Faith Beyond Beauty means to me — finding God's goodness in the places I never expected, and trusting Him to make something beautiful out of my breaking.

Wisdom Gained

That season taught me that faith is not just believing in God when life is good — it's trusting Him when nothing makes sense, when the nights feel endless, and when the weight of motherhood feels too heavy to carry. I learned that I didn't have to have it all together to be a good mother. God wasn't asking me to be perfect; He was asking me to depend on Him. That shift freed me from the pressure of trying to perform and allowed me to truly show up for my children — with grace, patience, and presence.

I also discovered that motherhood is not meant to be walked alone. Letting others in — whether through a prayer partner, a friend who listened, or a song that reminded me of God's promises — became part of my healing. God often uses community, scripture, and worship to strengthen us in our weakest moments.

If I could sit with another mama who feels weary and worn down right now, I would take her hands and tell her this:

"This is not permanent." The hard season you are in right now will pass. Don't miss the beauty in these moments by waiting for things to get easier. Lean into your faith. Allow God to meet you in the breaking, because it is there — in the raw and real moments — that He will show you just how strong and deeply loved you are.

Faith & Encouragement

Through that season, my faith became more than something I practiced on Sundays — it became the foundation I stood on every single day. When I felt like I was falling apart, God reminded me through His Word that I was never alone. The verse that carried me was Isaiah 41:10:

"Fear not, for I am with you; be not dismayed, for I am your God; I will strengthen you, I will help you, I will uphold you with my righteous right hand."

Every time I read those words, I felt Him lifting me up, reminding me that His strength was enough when mine ran out.

To the mama reading this who feels exhausted, unseen, or overwhelmed — take heart. Your faith does not have to be perfect for God to meet you where you are. All He asks is that you keep trusting Him, even in the small, shaky ways you can right now. Let worship be your weapon and prayer be your lifeline. He will carry you through this season, just like He did for me.

Remember this: the beauty of motherhood is not just in the perfect pictures or milestones — it is in the moments where you choose love over fear, faith over frustration, and hope over despair. Your story is still being written, and God is making something beautiful out of your breaking. Keep showing up, mama. You are not alone, and you are stronger than you know.

When the days feel long and the nights feel endless, pause and breathe deeply. Whisper a simple prayer:

"Lord, give me strength for this moment."

Write down one thing each day that you are grateful for — even if it's just, "I made it through today." These small practices shift your focus from what feels heavy to the quiet ways God is working on your behalf.

Remember, mama: you don't have to be perfect to be present. Keep choosing faith over fear, one small step at a time. Your love, your prayers, and your presence are shaping your children in ways that matter far beyond what you can see right now. You are doing holy, beautiful work — and God is with you every step of the way.

*Lord, thank You for meeting me in the breaking and for showing me that Your strength is made perfect in my weakness. Help me to keep choosing faith over fear and to see the beauty You are creating in every season of my life. I declare that I am equipped, I am enough, and I am never alone. Even in the hard and messy moments, I will trust You to carry me and my children forward. **Amen.***

Beauty in the Becoming: My Reflection

Devon Garrison

Devon Garrison is a passionate advocate for mothers, families, and the well-being of children. As a dedicated children's book author, she uses the power of storytelling to inspire, educate, and celebrate the experiences of young readers and their caregivers.

With years of hands-on experience as a **Newborn Care Specialist and Teacher,** Devon has guided countless families through the tender early stages of parenthood offering comfort, confidence, and expert support when it's needed most.

She is also a mother of two, the host of a **faith-based podcast**, where she leads heartfelt conversations about faith, healing, and resilience. She is also a Motivational Speaker as through every platform she touches, Devon's mission remains the same: to empower parents, nurture children, and strengthen the family bond.

Contact Information:

Instagram: Faithwalk_Podcast
          Magic_minds_books_
Tik Tok: Faithwalk Journey
          Magic_minds_books_

"Even in the valley of heartbreak, God is still writing my story."

MOMENTS FOR MOMS

Chapter Fourteen
Terrie Ann Polk
When a Mother's Heart Breaks

When we become mothers, we dream of a future filled with first steps, birthday parties, and graduations. We never imagine loss. In our hearts, we believe our children will one day bury us—not the other way around. Nothing prepares you for the moment you must live what you thought only happened to others.

I never imagined I'd become a grieving mother. It was never a path I thought I would walk. But life has a way of shifting the ground beneath us.

I am the proud mother of three beautiful children—Chrystal, my oldest and only daughter; Darius, my middle child and oldest son; and Jermaine, my baby. They are my greatest blessings and the best parts of me. But nothing could have prepared me for the day I lost my youngest, Jermaine, to violence.

When Jermaine was born, he brought so much love and joy into our lives. From the moment I held him, I knew he was special. He was my gentle giant—sweet, soft-spoken, and full of love. He adored his mama and loved his family deeply. Being the baby of the family, he was cherished by everyone. He had a calming presence and a big heart that touched everyone he met.

I still hear his deep voice: "Hey Mama, what you doing?" "Hey Mama, what you cooking?" I hold onto those words because they are pieces of him that will always stay with me.

Losing him shattered me. It felt like an emotional rollercoaster with no end—up, down, and turned inside out. The pain was unexplainable. Some days, I didn't think I would make it. Other days, I couldn't even get out of bed. I allowed myself space to grieve, to rest, and to be poured into. I didn't want to serve in ministry or speak the Word of God while broken and hurting. I needed to be healed. I needed God.
It was during this time that Proverbs 3:5–6 became my anchor. I didn't understand why this had to happen. I didn't want it. I questioned God. But one day, He answered me with a question of His own: "Why not you?"

God reminded me that what I was going through wasn't just for me. My pain would one day help another mother walk through hers. That became the hardest, yet most sacred chapter of my motherhood journey.

I find joy in remembering who my baby was—his love for food, sports, and knowledge. He loved to read, he knew God, and I'm thankful that this little boy with a big smile grew into an amazing man who will forever leave a mark on our hearts. His love and gentleness will last forever.

The Wisdom Gained

Grief doesn't follow a rulebook. It comes in waves. Some days are better than others. I've learned that healing doesn't mean forgetting—it means honoring your loved one while choosing to live again. My journey has been one day at a time, leaning into God for strength.

I also learned that I wasn't the only one grieving. My other two children, Chrystal and Darius, were hurting too. They had lost a part of themselves just as I had. I had to be intentional about checking in—asking how they were coping, listening without judgment, and encouraging them to hold on to their faith. I reminded them that there's no time limit on grief and no one right way to heal.

The hardest part as a mother was watching them hurt, knowing I couldn't take their pain away. I had to release them to God and trust Him to heal them just as He was healing me. Everyone's process was different, and that was okay.

I learned to love more deeply, encourage more consistently, and hold tighter to the bond we shared. Jermaine, being the baby, had been like a second child to his older siblings—almost as if they were his second set of parents. My daughter needed space to heal before she could pour into others, and my son had to find his footing again after losing not just his little brother, but also his best friend and co-worker. Through it all, I reminded them both to seek the Lord daily as they learned to live without Jermaine by their side.

Faith and Encouragement

Even in the darkest moments, God never left me. I felt His presence even when I was angry, even when I wanted to walk away. The same God who gave me 25 beautiful years with Jermaine is the same God who is restoring me day by day.

As Jermaine's mother and pastor, I had to deliver his eulogy. That was one of the hardest things I've ever done—sitting on the front row as a grieving mother, then standing to deliver a message of hope about my own child. Yet in that moment, I knew it wasn't my strength carrying me; it was God's. I had spoken faith, I had preached faith—now I had to walk faith.

Psalm 34:19 reminds us: *"Many are the afflictions of the righteous, but the Lord delivers him out of them all." That truth became my lifeline. Even through tears, I could still say, "God is faithful."*

Many told me I would never be the same, and they were right—but I also believe that God will stir something new in me. Out of pain, He brings purpose. Out of ashes, He brings beauty. I trust that He will heal me from the inside out and continue to use my life as a testimony of His faithfulness.

Purpose in the Pain

Grieving has taught me that if we love God, we can still live the rest of our lives as the gift He intended. God gave me a precious son and blessed me with 25 years to love, nurture, and pour into him. I have no regrets. I told my children daily that I loved them. I even had the chance to make amends for times I fell short as a mother—never realizing I was preparing myself for this very moment.
God knew what I would need. He is good, and I will serve Him for the rest of my life.

This journey has shown me not just who I am, but who He is—a faithful, all-powerful God who strengthens us to do what we never imagined we could. I stand on His promises, believing that even in loss, He is still writing my story.
To every grieving mother—God sees you. God knows your pain. Even in your tears, He's still working. What we've walked through may not make sense now, but one day, we will see purpose birth from pain. God can turn tragedy into testimony.

Take it one breath at a time. Don't rush your healing. Rest when you need to. Cry when you must. Be gentle with yourself. Don't let anyone tell you how to grieve. And never forget—your story, even the painful parts, has purpose.

Here's what I remind myself often: "This pain will not be wasted."
Write about your child. Speak their name. Keep their memory alive.
There is healing in remembrance. And when the world feels like it's
moving on without your baby, know that it's okay to still be holding on.

*Lord, thank You for walking with me through the valley. Strengthen
every mother whose heart has been broken. Remind her that even in
loss, there is life. Even in pain, there is purpose. Restore our joy, renew
our strength, and help us keep going—one day at a time.*
Amen.

Grief doesn't make you weak—it makes you real. It makes you tender.
It connects you to others in ways nothing else can. It's okay to not be
okay—for a while. Give yourself grace. Be honest with your emotions.
Cry without guilt. And trust that God is healing you, even when you can't
see it.

Purpose in the Pain: My Reflection

Terrie Ann Polk

Terrie Ann Polk is a mother of three—two living and one in heaven—and a proud grandmother of one. She holds a bachelor's degree in Business from Faulkner University and resides in Riverdale, Georgia. A prophetess, motivational speaker, author, businesswoman, and dedicated domestic violence advocate, Terrie uses her voice and testimony to help others heal, grow, and walk boldly in their God-given purpose.

As the author of *No More Tears: From Pain to Purpose*, Terrie's story is one of resilience and faith. She reminds us that even through heartbreak, God's grace has the final word.

Contact Information:

Email: Nomoretears56@gmail.com
Facebook: Terrie Ann

"God's goal was never just to give me a child — it was to give me testimony."

MOMENTS FOR MOMS

Chapter Fifteen
Dr. Yulanda Dante' West
My Momma Said and That Settles It

It was a very hot, humid July day in Bayou La Batre,
Alabama, when my momma said to me, "Don't call him your foster son
again. God says, "He's Your Son!"

You see, my husband (at the time) and I had struggled for seven long years to conceive. With the assistance of doctors, we were blessed with our son, Landon, born August 16, 1997. When Landon turned seven, he began longing for a sibling. We tried, prayed, and continued treatments, but another baby never came. After much discussion, we decided to become foster parents and see where God would lead us.

I had always believed in my mom's relationship with the Lord. I often called her 'Jesus' sister' because she never made a move or gave advice without going to the Bible, giving scriptures, and praying first. So her words to me did not fall on deaf ears. I internalized them deep in heart but quickly replied, "I know mom, but DHR's goal is to reunite the families, so I'm not getting attached."

With a warm smile she said, "God's goal is to give you the desires of your heart and he is your son."

We left my parents' home, and one week later, my mother passed away. It was the hardest thing I ever faced. It felt like a knife had been lodged in my heart, and I existed in constant pain. But through the throbbing hurt, I held on to her words: *"Don't introduce him as your foster son, God says he's your son."*

At that time, I had been married ten years. I was living in what I would call a season of *midnight*, when morning seemed to never come. Not only had my mother passed, but I longed for another son, and I was responsible for the care of my ill father. My emotions were a roller coaster- anger, grief, and confusion.

In my mind, God had called my mom home too soon. She was only 67, not yet the 70 years promised in Psalms 90:10. I remembered her dedication- praying, fasting, speaking in tongues, and trusting God. My dad even found her on the floor beside her bed with her Bible laid open, her daily routine before stepping into the day. She never left her room before spending time with the Lord, and asking, "What direction would you have me to go?'

Then I heard her voice, reminding me of her daily declaration: *"I live every day to go and be with Jesus."* God had given her the desires of her heart, and though she was gone, she still lived on through her words and example continued to live on through me.

During that midnight season of my life, I was 42 years old, and the youngest of three siblings and the only girl. The weight of caregiving and grieving fell squarely on my shoulders. But grieving, for me, wasn't an option. I had to put on my *big girl panties* (as they say) and keep it moving. My father, battling dementia and congestive heart failure, and needed my constant care.

All of this was unfolding while I was fostering, and praying that my sweet little boy would soon became a Clinton.

Now, in a moment of true transparency, I realized that my relationship with the Lord had largely been through my mother. It wasn't entirely my own. I began to seek Him personally, to call on Him, read His Word and develop my **_own_** personal relationship with the Lord. Boy did that help!

I can't lie and tell you that I even remember the exact scriptures that I read or prayers I prayed, but there are two that I always go to:

- Philippians 4:13 (KJV), *I can do all that can do all things through Christ who strengthens me.*

- Romans 8:28 (KJV), *"And we know that all things work together for good to those who love God, to those who are the called according to His purpose."*

If you didn't know, now you do- God truly causes everything to work together. (IYKYK. LOL)

Now back to our story: the adoption of my precious Justin.

It was a three-year journey. From day one to year three, I chose to live in the joy of anticipating his official addition to our family, even though it wasn't finalized. Yes, I will admit there were days when I feared we would have to return Justin to his birth mother, but most days we walked by faith, trusting God's Word and my mother's wisdom, and her unwavering faith in Him.

The process was stressful and exhausting. There were supervised visits with his birth mother, uncertainty and fear. But it taught me patience, faith, trust, and dependence on the Lord and His Word. I grew spiritually and emotionally, not only during the adoption process but also through the death of my mother and the eventual ending of my 20-year marriage. I had to step into the woman of God I was meant to be.

I began to read His Word, fast, pray, and spend time with Him, because I finally accepted that my mom wasn't God, and I had to know Him for myself. I once heard someone say that when you go through a test, it becomes your testimony, and that testimony will help someone else. are going through their test, it becomes their testimony, and their testimony will help someone else. My spiritual insight came not only through Justin's adoption but through the extended family God formed around us.

Before the adoption process could begin, all next of kin to had to be notified and given the opportunity to take him. None of Justin's maternal relatives came forward. His birth mother's rights were terminated for failing to meet the court's requirements, and his father's rights were terminated due to absence and illness. Only one paternal aunt came responded.

We met her for the first time, and though it was emotional, she became part of our village, supporting Justin and remaining a presence in our lives.

Now let me tell you about the God I came to know for myself.

Justin's aunt, an educator, "just happened" to be travelling to Mobile for a conference. She lived in Huntsville and was already raising two of Justin's older siblings, children he had never met, and who didn't even know he existed. In fact, his paternal family didn't know about Justin at all. His biological father lived in Birmingham with Justin's grandmother, caught up in a very undesirable life.

The social worker, Justin, and I met his aunt that day for the very first time. Justin sat very close to me, eventually resting in my lap where he felt safe and protected. The social worker led the meeting and explained that this might be Justin's last day with us. His aunt shared the situation with her brother (Justin's father), though meeting him for the first time, was willing to take him home.

I cried. Justin cried. The social worker cried. And his aunt cried. Then, with tears in her eyes, she said words I will never forget: "I can't take him from you, but please let him visit and learn his family."

In that moment, I saw God's hand clearly. We agreed that he was in the best place for him and that he would have a permanent family who loved him and could provide the stability care, and resources that he needed.

That was 23 years ago. Today, his aunt is like my sister from another mother. She has been there for every milestone in his life.

Justin faced many challenges. Diagnosed with learning disability, challenges with reading, needing speech therapy, and living with autism. He was developmentally delayed because of his birth mother's drug use during pregnancy. As an educator, I knew he wasn't ready for the third grade, so I made the decision to retain him to give him the foundation he needed to succeed.

He began the year in the second grade, but by the end of the first semester, it was clear he needed to move back to the first grade. After building confidence and skills, he advanced to second grade midway. That extra time gave him what he needed to succeed.

Here's the praise report: Justin made it to high school, graduated in 2018 with a 3.0 GPA, and earned a band scholarship to Mississippi Gulf Coast College! After his first year, he told me, "Mom college isn't for me." He came home, got a job, and is now working as an apprentice mechanic at a local car dealership. He has his own apartment, lives independently, and is thriving because God provided a village to surround him.

When I look back, I see that every "coincidence" was God's providence. Every challenge became a testimony of His faithfulness. And every tear we cried along the way was watering the seeds of joy we would later reap.

Encouragement for You:

Whether you are considering adoption, raising a child alone, or facing the loss of a loved one, remember:

"Trust in the LORD with all thine heart; and lean not unto thine own understanding. In all thy ways acknowledge him, and he shall direct thy paths." (Proverbs 3:5-6)

If you find yourself in this season or one similar hold fast to your faith, family and dearest friends. Never give up.

"But seek ye first the kingdom of God, and his righteousness; and all these things shall be added unto you." (Matthew 6:33)

Even when grief or trials come, joy will follow:
"Weeping may endure for a night but joy cometh in the morning." (Psalms 30:5)

And remember, take care of yourself while taking care of others. Self-perseverance is a must.

If you don't have an exercise routine create one. For me, running was the time for **me**. I would run a minimum of three miles a day, seven days a week outside, breathing in God's air. You may not be a runner but whatever you choose, be consistent and intentional to make it happen.

Find and read scriptures of encouragement, and strength and remind God of His Word. Those that I have mentioned above are just a few of the ones I hold fast to.

Blessing and Peace to you!

When Obedience Births Miracles: My Reflection

Dr. Yulanda Dante' West

Dr. Yulanda Dante' West is a retired educator with more than 34 years of dedicated service in the field of education. Her passion for students and learning has been evident throughout her career, which began as an elementary school teacher and culminated in her role as a college professor.

A native of Bayou La Batre, Alabama, Dr. West was raised by her late parents, Delores and Robert West, alongside her two older brothers. She is the proud mother of three sons—Lemuel Jr., Landon, and Justin—and the delighted grandmother (Ya-Ya) of two: Autumn Rose Clinton, an energetic 8-year-old third grader, and Apollo LeMonte Clinton, now six months old.

Dr. West earned her Bachelor of Science (Elementary Ed.), Master's (Elementary Education), and Education Specialist (Ed.S.) School Counseling degrees from the University of South Alabama and later achieved her Ph.D. in Educational Administration from the University of Southern Mississippi.

Throughout her distinguished career in the Mobile County Public School System, she served as a first- and second-grade teacher, an elementary, middle, and high school counselor, a secondary assistant principal, and a middle school principal. She retired from the system in 2018, but her love for education led her back to the classroom the following year as a professor at Talladega College in Talladega, Alabama.

Now residing in Mobile, Alabama, Dr. West remains active in her church and community. She enjoys traveling, shopping, spending time with her family, reading, laughing, loving, and living life to the fullest.

Contact Information:

Facebook – Dr. Yulanda West
LinkedIn – Yulanda Clinton, Ph.D.
Email: drywc48@gmail.com

"I had to love myself before I could teach my children what love truly is."

MOMENTS FOR MOMS

Chapter Sixteen
Tonisha Morton
Healing from within while Breaking
Generational Curses as a mother

Breaking generational curses began the moment I could look my children in the eyes and say, *"I love you,"* without fear or discomfort. Those words felt foreign to me. Growing up, I never heard them. *"I love you"* was a ghost, and hugs were nonexistent. Affection was silenced, and for a long time, I didn't realize how deeply that shaped me.

I just knew I wanted to be better, even if I didn't know what "better" looked or felt like. But every time I tried to say, **"I love you"**, it felt empty because I hadn't healed yet. I hadn't yet found my voice. I was still holding on to the pain of the past. Still trapped in generational cycles I didn't even know existed.

154

It wasn't until I started doing the hard work facing both past and present trauma that I uncovered a truth I had been avoiding: I didn't truly love myself. I was living in the middle of a generational curse, whether I chose it or not. This was my reality.

I was broken and damaged, carrying wounds from childhood into adulthood. The truth was, I had to break those curses in order to become the woman and mother I had prayed to be. Healing taught me that love starts within, that my voice matters, and that *"I love you"* is more than a phrase. It is a declaration of growth, courage, transformation, and genuine feeling. Now, when I say it to my children, it comes from a place of truth, confidence, and trust. Not survival.

Healing from generational trauma is essential for personal growth and for the generations that follow. By embracing self-love, I empower myself to break cycles of pain and create spaces where healing can flourish.

> *"Train up a child in the way he should go: and when he is old, he will not depart from it."* — *Proverbs 22:6.*

I'm not someone who memorizes many Bible verses, but for some reason, this one stayed with me. I've often wondered why. Looking back, I believe God embedded it in my heart because it would become the foundation for how I raised my children. It would be the scripture that helped me set me apart from the bondage, trauma, and pain of my past, guiding me toward pouring into the children God allowed me to birth.

At twelve years old, I became a victim of sexual assault. Statistics states that 60% of Black girls report experiencing sexual assault by that age, and nearly half of the abusers are family members. Many never report it, silenced by fear, shame, or disbelief. For me, those conversations never happened, before or after the abuse.

When I became a mother, I prayed constantly for open, honest communication with my children. I wanted us to talk about everything, even uncomfortable things. I made a conscious decision to be the voice for my children until they could find their own.

I was overlooked when I spoke my truth, made to feel invisible and manipulated into silence. That pain caused me to hate love, men, fathers, God, and even myself. But in the quiet of my pain, I made a vow to God, myself, and my children, that I would break every generational curse that had been handed to me.

Patterns of negative behavior, trauma, or misfortune often pass silently from one generation to the next. These generational curses can show up in many forms — cycles of abuse, unhealthy relationships, poor communication, financial struggles, and even unaddressed mental and physical issues. Once I accepted that I was living out patterns I had inherited, I was able to seek the help I desperately needed to heal.

Through that journey, I learned how deeply rooted sexual assault is within the African American community. My own commitment to God and my children pushed me to speak openly, from the heart, about my experiences. I believe every mother should consider having these hard but life-saving conversations with their children. Sharing the truth about your past, the very experiences that shaped you, could protect them from walking through the same pain.

The road to self-love often starts with facing difficult truths about our past. Many of us unknowingly carry the weight of childhood wounds into adulthood, repeating patterns of emotional and psychological distress. While I never put my children in environments that would directly cause them trauma, I was still living in my own hurt, and that pain sometimes reflected found its way into my parenting.

It became clear: breaking the cycle would require deep change within myself. I committed to the hard work, both in therapy and through spiritual growth, for years. Healing demanded that I address my mental and emotional wounds head-on, so my children could inherit something better. Hope, love, and a healthier future.

I began to see my healing as a steppingstone toward becoming the woman and mother I always prayed to be. My children can openly say they've witnessed my journey of self-love, healing and breaking generational curses. That, in itself, is a powerful lesson in resilience and transformation. It was in these moments that Proverbs 22:6 became real to me:, *Train up a child in the way he should go: and when he is old, he will not depart from it.*

By God's grace, I've been able to teach my children principles, values, truth, morals, and self-love, all while walking through my own process of breaking generational curses. I've shown them that healing is not weakness; it's strength.

Moms, breaking generational curses is never easy, but it is possible. And the freedom you find on the other side is worth every step. Throughout my journey, my children watched even on the days I thought they weren't paying attention. By keeping an open and honest relationship with them, I unknowingly gave them tools for their own lives.

I saw this firsthand when my child, at just twelve years old, spoke up in an uncomfortable situation in a way I could only have dreamed of doing at that age That courage, that voice, was born out of the generational curses I refused to pass down.

By leaning into my faith, I have discovered new perspectives, healing practices, and community support that helped me break free from negative patterns and cycles that have persisted in my family. I had to trust God, though at the time, I didn't truly know what that meant or what it looked like. I didn't trust a single human being, and learning to trust a God I couldn't see felt impossible.

I wasn't taught to be a faithful servant. But my God, when I learned to walk by faith and not by sight, my whole world shifted. The shackles fell with every single step. I remember praying asking God to remove anything or anyone that was blocking me from being close to Him. And He did,.

Thank you God, I have to shout it out! Because of His grace and mercy, I am able to share my story so t another mother can become the vessel God uses to set her free. Free of trauma free. Free from shame. Free from self-hate. Free of generational curses.

"And God is faithful; he will not let you be tempted beyond what you can bear. But when you are tempted, he will also provide a way out so that you can endure it." – 1 Corinthians 10:13.

God has given me the ability to turn my pain into purpose, not just for my children, but for anyone who needs to see that it's possible to trust again. I will take their hand and walk with them as they begin their journey.

As you read this, know that the journey of healing from generational curses may feel uncertain, but it is not only possible, it is life-changing. Your courage to confront this cycle not just healing you; is building a new legacy for your children, one that will be filled with love, peace, and freedom. By breaking the cycle, lifting the burden, and creating a beautiful path for generations to come, you are opening doors freedom that will never close.

Stay committed to your journey. Trust that even the smallest shifts can grow into the greatest legacy. I pray that this brings confirmation, and peace, reminding you that you are not alone, and that through God, it is possible.

Breaking the Cycle: My Reflection

Tonisha Morton

Tonisha Morton, born in Washington, D.C., Tonisha Morton is a devoted mother and woman of faith whose life reflects resilience, purpose, and love. As the eldest of her siblings, she learned early the importance of leadership and responsibility—qualities that have shaped her journey through motherhood and personal growth.

After welcoming her three children—a daughter in 2007 and two sons in 2008 and 2019—Tonisha discovered her greatest calling: nurturing and guiding the next generation. In 2020, she made the courageous decision to relocate her family to Raleigh, North Carolina, to pursue greater opportunities and break generational barriers. Since then, she has coauthored the bestselling book *Moments for Moms, Volume 1*, and is a proud recipient of the **2025 Moments for Moms Legacy Award**.

Tonisha's journey continues to be a testament to faith, perseverance, and the power of a mother's love to create lasting legacy.

Contact Information:

Email: Tonishamorton@gmail.com
Instagram: SincerelyTonisha
Facebook: Tonisha Morton

"I used to think my scars made me less beautiful. Now I see they make me unbreakable."

MOMENTS FOR MOMS

Chapter Seventeen
Jvonne Belle
A Mama with Trauma

Imagine waking up on your birthday gasping for air and with each passing moment, it gets worse.

According to, Google *"Psychological trauma is a severe emotional response to a stressful event that overwhelms a person's ability to process it emotionally. It can be caused by direct or indirect experiences, such as accidents, natural disasters, war zones, bodily injury, or sexual violence."*

We've all experienced some type of trauma within our lives, and adding motherhood on top of trauma that hasn't been addressed, can feel like a circus. Where do we find the time for therapy? We barely have time to heal, to be vulnerable, or to care for ourselves. As a mother, I'm always putting my child before myself. That selfless act can become exhausting and stressful, especially when you're trying not to fall apart. Personally, I'm still unpacking a ton of trauma. God has been leading me the through it all, but I still fall sometimes when it comes to Him.

Not being able to catch my breath had to be one of the most scariest moments of my life. My oxygen had dropped below 50, and it was almost unbearable to breathe. Long story short, I ended up on ECMO, was moved through four different hospitals, became paralyzed, had a tracheotomy, died during the journey, and developed a stage 4 bed sore.

Whewww! At this point I'm a walking billboard for trauma. At the time, my daughter was only eight. The last time she saw me, to her, I looked normal. By the next time she saw me again, I had so many machines attached to me that she had to sidestep into the room. It scared the daylights out of her, but she was such a big helper during her visit, she even gave me my meds.

When I was finally able to return home, I was loaded with anxiety, anger, and depression. I no longer looked like or felt like myself. I had lost all of my hair from chemo, which was used as a form of treatment for my lupus and scleroderma.

Appearance had always been important to me, and suddenly, I was fifty pounds lighter, my skin was darker, and I had a wound vac attached to my tailbone. Needless to say, I couldn't control my emotions. I was a ticking time bomb waiting to explode. Anyone who looked at me too long, spoke too loudly, or even looked like they were having fun….made me so angry!

Living with lasting trauma is a full time job. Every day, I use a breathing exercises just to remain calm or to bring myself down from triggers. And I do all of this while trying to keep it together for my baby. Most of time, she catches the bad end of the stick because it's just the two of us at home. Anytime I take my frustration out on her, I feel terrible, but my baby is so understanding. She always gives me a big hug and reminds me, *"It's going to be ok."*

I am truly grateful to have such an amazing daughter. She saw firsthand what I went through and how hard I fought to find my new normal. What would I do without her? I endured some of the most horrible treatment while lying in some of those hospital beds! From laying in my own waste for hours, having my help button disabled, and being told "no" when asking for assistance. Those experiences led me to seek Prolonged Exposure Therapy.

In Prolonged Exposure therapy we tackle two parts: Imaginal therapy (where I relive the trauma repeatedly in my head and out aloud) and Vivo Exposure Therapy (where I confront safe situations that I have been avoiding because I became nervous about them after my trauma). Because of what I've been through, I often avoid certain places, situations, or activities my appearance due to having thirty-two new beauty marks. To my family and friends, I'm Super-Woman, but sometimes I suffer in silence so that I don't appear weak.

I preach God, self-worth, and confidence to my daughter all the time, yet I fall short for myself. Rylee, my daughter, keeps me accountable. Whether it's taking my medicine, reminding me to show affection, or to simply have fun. I don't take her for granted, and I'm very transparent with her. She knows I struggle with living in the past, of what happened to me, but she also knows I'm going to show up for her daily even when I may not feel like myself.

Some of the most common problems after trauma are fear, anxiety, avoidance, grief, and depression. I often blame myself for things I did or didn't do to survive. I felt like I put up the fight of the century, but I also lost a huge part of myself during the process.

As a mother I fall short more days than I like to admit due to my past trauma. Healing takes time and honesty, and I'm learning to give myself both. Isaiah 40:29 *"He give strength to the weary and increases the power of the weak"* During my weakest moments, God always steps in and strengthens me. Through every trial, I've learned to embrace each moment as it comes and give myself grace. It's ok to feel, it's ok to cry, and it's okay to not be okay.

Life is such a beautiful journey filled with so many ups and downs. Motherhood adds a new level of compassion, love, strength, and perspective. You discover parts of yourself that you never knew existed when a little person is depending on you.

Isaiah 42:10 *"Do not fear, for I am with you; do not be dismayed, for I am your God. I will strengthen you and help you; I will uphold you with my righteous right hand."*

When You're Having a Rough Day:

Inhale a slow deep breath foe three seconds, your heart needs a moment to breathe and pause. Exhale gently for six seconds. You should start to feel the release of the weight you were carrying.

If you can, step outside and place your feet on the grass so you feel grounded.

Most importantly, pray. Ask od to give you strength! Your trauma doesn't define who you are, but it will help you find your purpose in life.

If you're reading this and you're in your own storm, know that you're not alone! Trust in God with all your heart believe that he will see you through and it shall be done!

I'll leave you with my favorite scripture:

"With God all things are possible!" Matthew 19:26

Grace for the Healing Mama: My Reflection

Jvonne Belle

Jvonne Belle grew up in the small town of Springfield, South Carolina. She is the proud mother of a beautiful daughter, Rylee, who is the light of her world. Jvonne earned her bachelor's degree in Business Administration with a concentration in Management from the University of South Carolina Aiken. A newly published author of *My Last Breath*, makeup artist, and full-time corporate professional, Jvonne continues to pursue her passions while inspiring others to do the same. In her spare time, she enjoys traveling and creating new memories with her daughter.

Contact Information:

Facebook: Jvonne Belle
Email: jvonnebelle@gmail.com

"A mother's strength isn't in knowing everything – it's in trusting the One who does."

MOMENTS FOR MOMS

Chapter Eighteen
Ebony S. Bailey
Trusting God When Their Words Run Out

The transition from childhood to the teenage years is something nobody really prepares you for. It is a stretch of motherhood that can feel like walking in the dark, one hand reaching for your child and the other lifted to heaven, asking God to help you understand.

Our children are still young in many ways, but they are growing up in a world that offers them more than we ever had to carry at their age. They see things sooner. They have access to information we did not at their age. Their eyes and ears are wide open to influences that reach far past what we can control inside our homes. And even still, they are just children. They are learning, growing, stumbling, and trying to find words for feelings they do not even understand yet.

I felt this deeply with my middle daughter. I am a mom of five. Two boys and three girls. Each one is so different and so beautifully unique. My oldest and youngest are boys with my three girls sandwiched in the middle, each of them carrying their own light, struggles, and ways of moving through the world.

When my daughter started to shift, you know, that change you cannot name but you feel in your spirit, I could not put my finger on it. She was quieter. Something was off. Her influences were stretching beyond my four walls, beyond church, beyond the things I tried so hard to protect her from.

So I did what I always do. I stayed before the Lord. I prayed, God, show me what I cannot see. Let her open up to me in a way that makes sense. Help me not to miss what is happening. I stood on James 1:5 (NIV): "If any of you lacks wisdom, you should ask God, who gives generously to all without finding fault, and it will be given to you." I leaned on that promise as I waited.

One day she did open up, but not in the way I expected. She did not have all the words, but she knew enough to say, Mama, can I talk to a therapist? I felt proud and sad all at the same time. I wanted her to come to me, to feel safe enough to lay it all out on my lap. But I was so grateful she recognized she needed help. She could not carry it alone, and she wanted to let it out to someone who could help her sort through it all.

So I stepped aside. I let her get what she needed from somewhere else. And I thanked God for the reminder that sometimes loving our children well means letting them have another voice in their corner.

That experience taught me a deeper level of trust. Trust that God is parenting alongside me. Trust that when my understanding falls short, His Spirit speaks. Trust that when my child needs a word, I do not have, He will bring the right people to pour into her.

I hold onto Proverbs 3:5-6 (NIV): *"Trust in the Lord with all your heart and lean not on your own understanding. In all your ways submit to Him and He will make your paths straight."* That includes the paths my children are walking, even the ones I cannot see.

It also showed me that I have to keep creating space for my kids to be honest about what they feel, even if they cannot fully explain it to me. I had to let go of the idea that a perfectly open house means they will tell me everything. Some things they cannot process yet. Some things are too heavy to say out loud to the person they love most. And that is okay.

What matters is that they know they can talk. They can be quiet. They can process. They can grow. They can ask for someone else to help, and I will not make them feel guilty for it.

When I struggle, I remind myself of Isaiah 54:13 (NKJV): *"All your children shall be taught by the Lord, and great shall be the peace of your children."* I might not have all the answers, but I trust that He is teaching them even when I cannot reach them.

Philippians 4:13 (NKJV) says, *"I can do all things through Christ who strengthens me."* That includes mothering kids in a generation that is exposed to so much so fast. That includes holding my tongue when I want to push for answers they are not ready to give. That includes trusting that the same God who loves me loves them more, and He is fully capable of guiding them into healing, sometimes through my voice and sometimes through someone else's. I also stand on Psalm 121:7-8 (NIV): *"The Lord will keep you from all harm. He will watch over your life. The Lord will watch over your coming and going both now and forevermore."* I pray this over my children by name. When I cannot be everywhere, He is.

To every mama reading this, I want you to know you are not failing when your child needs more than you. You are growing. They are growing. You are building trust with them and with God. It is holy work. Continue to create space for your kids to process, express themselves, and feel. Let them know they are seen and remind them that their voice matters.

Assure your children that they are allowed to need help, even if it is not from you. This is big! Do not let pride get in the way of your child's healing. That will create unnecessary trauma they should not have to deal with, all because you want to control something you were never designed to. When they cannot find the words, be the safe place that says it is okay. We will figure it out together. And if you need someone else, I will stand right here while you do.

As I continue walking through this season, here are a few practical things that are helping me:

- I give myself grace daily, remembering that I am learning right alongside my children.
- I choose to be honest about my emotions instead of keeping them to myself in silence.
- I remind myself not to suffer internally when, often, a simple conversation can shift everything.
- I start small talks with my kids, even if they are short, because silence does not mean failure; it very well may mean they are processing.
- I make space for my own outlet, whether through journaling, prayer, therapy, or trusted friends, so I can pour from a full cup.
- I pray scripture over each of my children by name because it steadies my heart and covers their lives. I dress them in the Spirit until they know how to do it on their own.
- I invite help without guilt, trusting that safe voices outside of me can still reinforce what God is doing in our home.

These are some of the things that keep me grounded and remind me God's grace meets me here, day by day.

When we have done this we will show even more of our humanity to our children. Yes, we wear our capes (some days better than others), but we also know how to take them off and release! In the process, your children will grow up remembering that they were seen, heard, and loved for exactly who they are, not just for who you want them to be. They will know that it is safe to reach out to ask for help to heal. And they will carry that strength with them for the rest of their lives.

*Lord, thank You for being the gap filler when my parenting feels incomplete. Give me eyes to see, ears to hear, and a heart that trusts You fully with every part of my children's lives. Remind me daily that You alone are their keeper and teacher. Surround them with the right voices, the right safe spaces, and the courage to become exactly who You created them to be. Let them feel your warmth, guidance, and more as they grow. Your word reminds us that if we train up a child in the way they should go when they are old, they won't depart from it. So I trust You, Lord, with my children; I release them into Your capable hands. In Jesus' Name, **Amen**.*

Letting Go, Letting God:
My Reflection

Ebony S. Bailey

Ebony S. Bailey is an award-winning author, publisher, speaker, and empowerment strategist dedicated to helping individuals awaken to their purpose and walk in it ON purpose. As the visionary behind the She Woke Up movement, she challenges women to rise above fear, doubt, and stagnation to create the life they were designed to live.

In 2024, Ebony was honored with the DWAP Award for Innovator of the Year, recognizing her groundbreaking contributions to publishing, empowerment, and personal development. As the founder of Purposely Booked Publishing, she helps aspiring and established authors bring their voices and visions to print. With over 18 years of experience in administrative roles, she has mastered the art of creating efficient systems and guiding others through the publishing process with clarity and confidence.

Her work extends beyond books—she curates life-changing experiences through The She Woke Up Creating Conference, The She Woke Up Web Series, and her motivational journals and guided planners under Dreampad.

As a certified life coach, Ebony is passionate about helping others overcome obstacles that hold them back from living fully in their purpose. She has spoken at numerous women's events and featured in Bold Journey Magazine and Canvas Rebel Magazine. Her voice is amplified through The Unscripted Push Podcast, where she and co-host DeVonnda Shantel have raw, unfiltered conversations about faith, family, business, and personal growth.

Ebony's signature event, The She Woke Up Creating Conference, is a two-day experience that equips women to build, grow, and dominate their God-given assignments. In 2025, the conference theme, "She Woke Up Dominating," encourages attendees to enter a season of strategic execution and mastery in business, leadership, and personal development.

Beyond conferences and publishing, Ebony is a devoted wife, mother of five, and a woman of faith who believes in the power of storytelling to transform lives. She continues to inspire others through her books, courses, and speaking engagements, reminding them that their voice has value—and it's time to wake up and use it.

Contact Information:

Email: ebony@purposelybooked.com
Instagram: @SheWokeUpCon |
@ebsbailey
Website: ebonysbailey.com

"Even far from everything familiar, His Word was my comfort."

MOMENTS FOR MOMS

Chapter Nineteen
Debbie Luckett
Home Is Where My Heart Is

They said, "Be careful what you ask for!" But as a young adult, I did not listen. So many times, we hear the words of our elders with our ears but not our hearts. We perceive our world from a child's mind with no clue to the reality of the adult world. Even school and Sunday school can't teach us to see what we have not yet experienced.

I grew up believing that the world was like my community, and that people were interested in my perspective and my happiness. I soon found out how small my world was as compared to the real world!

At 19, I traveled to Virginia from my home in Wisconsin and never returned. I took the opportunity to get away from family and the farm to start a new life in the beautiful city of Hampton. I had met a young man from church who invited me to visit his home and family. Why not? I was young, single, and full of dreams! What I didn't know then, I was all alone in a foreign land; with only God to guide me.

The young man became my husband, and we made our home about fifteen minutes from his parents. We got married like nine months after my arrival, and for a while, life was fun. We shared many interests, and we enjoyed road trips to various towns in Virginia and North Carolina. We were both firstborns and raised in the same faith, so by all appearances, church. life should have been ideal. However, deeper comparison would find a few distinct differences.

A year later, I was getting ready to give birth to our first child. I got along well with his parents, but our family dynamics were worlds apart. His family lives in the city with two children; mine lived on a 160-acre dairy farm, and I was the oldest of thirteen. I attended a Christian school; and he went to public school. Both families prayed, but my parents' faith ran deeper. My mom gave birth to most of us at home and trusted God for all things medical, while his family went to the doctor for everything. Since I was now living in his world, I would give birth in the hospital. That opened a whole new perspective on trusting God.

My labor started on Sunday afternoon. We were at his parents' house for dinner. I went ahead and to be polite, even though I suspected I might be in labor. My mom would have told me that it was a bad idea to eat meatloaf and green peas during contractions, and I soon learned why. By the time I got to the hospital, I was throwing it all up!

I had never been admitted to a hospital before. Now I was in pain, sick to my stomach, and scared of all the unknowns of the "evil hospital". I had to learn a new way of trusting God to guide other humans for my care, instead of trusting Him to care for me directly as I had been taught.

The birth of my son went well, but the next day, when I thought we were ready to go home, the nurses said my baby couldn't come home yet. I was devastated. I had no idea what jaundice was; all of us were born at home. My heart was absolutely shattered to go home without my baby. He was released the following day, but I will never forget the shock I felt that night. Complete strangers were in control of caring for my newborn son, and I had no choice but to trust them. My faith in God had to grow deeper to survive this new reality.

Once my baby came home, I was on my own. I knew how to help with babies, but being solely responsible for that tiny person was totally different than being a big sister. My husband was afraid and unwilling to hold him and believed babies were a woman's job. His mother helped when she could, but she had a full-time job, so we only saw her on the weekend. I talked to my mom on the phone for breastfeeding advice and moral support, but it was too far to travel for a visit. It was just me and my little boy. I was so far away from my home and out of my element; I was too scared to know I was scared, too naive to realize I needed my own mother during this time.

The beacon of hope during this dark hour was the scriptures I had memorized while enrolled in Christian school. My favorite verse is Psalm 23:4, *"Yea, though I walk through the valley of the shadow of death, I will fear no evil, For Thou art with me; thy rod and thy staff they comfort me."*

Hanging on tight to God has brought me safely through this season and many more dark days in my life that followed. That season was the darkest test I had ever faced in my young life. I had plenty of time to talk to God while rocking and nursing my baby. I developed my very own personal relationship with Him and He carried me thru the valley.

Looking back, I would recommend any young woman to stay in close contact with her parents after she leaving home. I know it's not always affordable or even possible, but I could have leaned on my mother much more. I was never particularly close to my mother because I was usually outside with my father. Most of my conversations growing up were with him, but even then, I missed out. I didn't think I needed her so much, but looking back, my life would have been easier with more of her wisdom to guide me.

In that season, I learned what it meant to depend on God for real—not just in theory, but in the everyday moments when I felt like I didn't know what I was doing. *"The Lord is my rock and my fortress and my deliverer; my God, my strength, in whom I will trust…"* Psalm 18:2. I learned that God's Grace is sufficient for all my struggles. He has all of the answers for me that I thought I had.

It's okay to feel weak in certain seasons of our lives. It's not okay to try to get through it alone – and not necessary. Reach out to your mom, auntie, sister, cousin, friend and most of all, Jesus.

I no longer have the option to reach out to my mom, as she has home to be with Jesus. But I still have God, family, and new friends to lean on for strength in time of need.

Lord, thank You for walking with me through every new beginning. Even when I was far from home, Your Words reminded me that I was never far from Your presence. Help every mama reading this to lean into Your comfort and know that You are with her, no matter where she is. **Let this season draw her closer to** You. **Amen.**

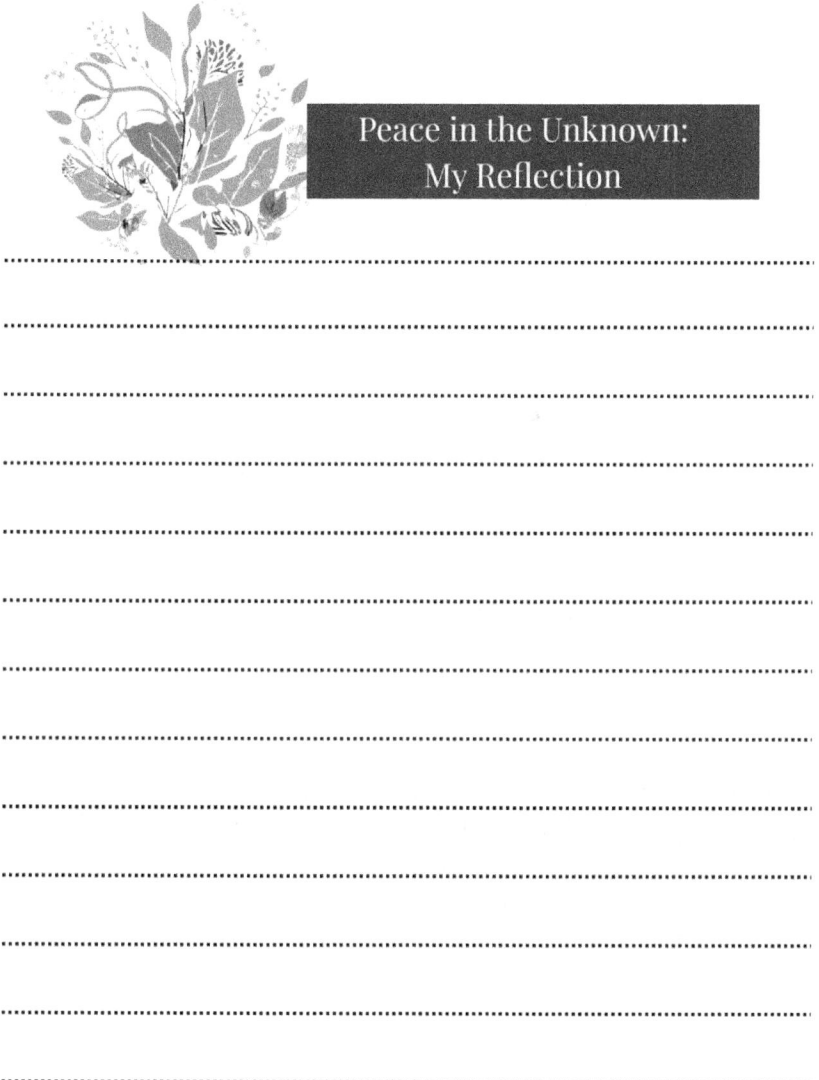

Peace in the Unknown:
My Reflection

....

....

....

....

....

....

....

....

....

....

....

....

Debbie Luckett

Debbie Luckett was born in Rice Lake, Wisconsin, at the tail end of the Baby Boom generation. She grew up in a small country church, where her love for faith and community was nurtured. Now residing in Southern California, Debbie remains actively involved in her local church and continues to live out her purpose through service and love.

A devoted caregiver, teacher, wife, mother, and proud grandmother of fourteen, Debbie finds joy in family, faith, and simple moments of creativity. She enjoys sewing, gardening, and sharing her life experiences to inspire others. *Moments for Moms, Volume 4* marks her debut as a published author.

Contact Information:

Email: 1ladyluckett@gmail.com
Facebook: Debbie Ellen Luckett

"Light is still there, even when you can't see it."

MOMENTS FOR MOMS

Chapter Twenty
Joi West Phalo
What Does Hope At The End of The Tunnel
Look Like for You?

Can you remember a time where you have actually made it to the end of a tunnel with hope?

Hope at the end of the tunnel doesn't always come in big, life-changing moments. Sometimes, it's as simple as a quiet night of rest, a child's laugh after a hard day, or the strength to keep going when you feel like giving up. It can be found in a kind word, a friend's support, or a small smile that reminds you—you're not alone.

However hope reveals itself in your life, I pray this chapter—and this book—brings you one step closer to finding your own hope at the end of the tunnel. Light is still there, even when you can't see it.

Although I believed in hope, there were many times it felt like it was taking me forever to reach the destination I had in mind.

For me, hope at the end of the tunnel looked like this...

The Moment Everything Changed....

I was only fifteen when I found out I was pregnant. Still a child myself—full of dreams, fears, and insecurities—suddenly responsible for another human. I remember the exact night my mom went to the store and brought home two pregnancy tests. She handed them to me gently but firmly, with that look only a mother can give.

"Take one now," she said, "and we'll do the other in the morning."

That night, I sat in the bathroom, my heart pounding. When the two little pink lines appeared, I stood there in shock. I was speechless! What now? What will my parents do? How can I do this? I placed the test on the counter, staring at it as if the little plastic stick could give me all the answers.

The next morning, I took the second test. Positive again. My mom's reaction wasn't what I expected. Honestly, I don't even know what I was expecting—maybe anger, maybe disappointment, maybe embarrassment. Instead, she seemed quiet, almost in shock herself.

A few days later, after everything was confirmed at the doctor and I began prenatal care, she said words I will never forget: "Don't worry. We are going to help you raise this baby so that you can graduate from high school."

And she meant it. She didn't just speak encouragement; she put action behind it. She hired a nanny to care for my son while I was in school. She made sure I had time to finish my homework, even if that meant her staying up late with me. She was determined that my future wasn't over just because my path looked different.

Life as a Teen Mom

Being a PK (preachers kid) and the daughter of a school counselor, I know people whispered. Some judged. Others turned away. But a few precious souls leaned in, wrapped me in love, and reminded me I was still worthy of a future.

Still, the road ahead looked long and overwhelming. I didn't know how to be a mother when I was still trying to figure out how to be me.

The early days were brutal. Sleepless nights with a newborn. Waking up every two to three hours to feed, yet still determined to get out of bed for school the next morning. I remember sitting in class, my body present but my mind exhausted, thinking about my future.

My friends were going to homecoming, prom, football games, and parties. I was home rocking a baby to sleep, folding laundry, and learning how to mix formula bottles. There were nights I would cry quietly after my son finally fell asleep, whispering questions into the dark: *Why me? How did I let this happen? Will I ever get my life back?* But even in my tears, I knew giving up wasn't an option.

Determined Not to Be a Statistic

I kept telling myself, *I want more for my son. I want more for myself.*

Society already had a label ready for me: teen mom. Statistic. Failure. But I was determined with everything in me, that this would not be the end of my story.

I wanted my son to grow up proud of his mother, not ashamed of her. That determination became my fuel.

Being a teen mom taught me more than any textbook ever could. It made me stronger. It made me more determined. And it showed me the beauty of unconditional love—the kind of love that sacrifices, that endures, that gives even when it feels empty.

Lessons from the Hard Days

Motherhood at fifteen taught me truths I even carry now:

- **Presence matters more than perfection.** I didn't always get it right, but I did what I had to do, and that was enough.

- **Shame loses power when you speak your truth.** Silence keeps you bound, but honesty sets you free.

- **Life may not look how you imagined, but it can still be sacred and beautiful.** God brings purpose out of pain.

There were countless moments I didn't feel strong enough—but God was.

Clinging to God's Promises

One scripture became my anchor:

"So do not fear, for I am with you; do not be dismayed, for I am your God. I will strengthen you and help you; I will uphold you with my righteous right hand."
— Isaiah 41:10

I clung to those words on sleepless nights, during anxious mornings, and when the weight of my reality felt too heavy to carry.

Slowly, I realized God wasn't punishing me—He was preparing me. He was drawing me closer, building strength I didn't know I had, and shaping me into the woman I would one day become.

Encouragement for Other Moms

If you're a mom—especially a young mom—reading this and feeling overwhelmed, I want you to know:

- You are not your mistakes.
- You are not broken.
- You are chosen, loved, and capable of incredible things.

God sees you. He hears your silent prayers and collects every tear. Your story isn't over—it's just unfolding.

When the tunnel feels endless, take it one step at a time. Rest when you need to. Ask for help when it feels too heavy. And remember:

- You are allowed to grow and heal at your own pace.

- You are not disqualified from purpose because of a difficult beginning.

- You are closer to the light with every step you take.

A Little Tip: Keep a "Hope Journal." On the hardest days, write down one small blessing—a baby's giggle, a kind text, a scripture that speaks to you. Looking back will remind you that even in the dark, God was present.

A Prayer and Blessing

Lord, thank You for meeting me in the midst of my struggles and never letting go. Thank You for the gift of motherhood, even when it comes in unexpected seasons.

I lift up every mother reading this right now:

- *For the young mom who feels alone, remind her she is never truly alone—you are with her.*

- *For the tired mom who feels like giving up, breathe new strength into her spirit.*

- *For the mom carrying shame, replace it with grace.*

- *For the one questioning her future, whisper to her that her story is still being written.*

Cover every child represented by these mothers. Surround them with love, safety, and purpose. And remind every mother that there is hope— even when the tunnel feels long and dark.

*In Jesus' name, **Amen.***

Always remember this: *If I got through it, you can too.*

Your story isn't over, and your light is still shining—even if you can't see it yet.

Light in the Tunnel: My
Reflection

....

....

....

....

....

....

....

....

....

....

....

....

Joi West Phalo

Joi West Phalo is an author, speaker, and advocate with a heart for empowering teen moms and women. Originally from Mobile, Alabama, she now lives in Charleston, South Carolina, with her husband, Derrick. Together, they are the proud parents of four children and lead a marriage ministry called We Change Everything, focused on building faith-filled, purpose-driven relationships.

Joi is also the founder of She Changes Everything and co-host of the Hope at the End of the Tunnel Podcast. She has written seven books and was featured on The Jennifer Hudson Show in 2023, where one of her inspirational quotes from her debut novel, 15.19.23., was highlighted during a special "Coffee Mug Moment."

In 2023, Joi was honored as a Distinguished Author of Alabama, and in 2024, she received the Inspiring Women of the Gulf Coast award.

Through her powerful testimony, unwavering faith, and dedication to uplifting families and communities, Joi continues to inspire others to walk boldly into their purpose.

Contact Information:

Website: www.joiwestphalo.com
Email: Shechanges1@gmail.com
Facebook: Joi West Phalo/ She Changes
Everything
Instagram: @author_jphalo

"Motherhood and mission were never meant to cancel each other out."

MOMENTS FOR MOMS

Twenty-One
Juanita Nicole Woodson
The Quiet Season

I never imagined that a quiet season could feel so loud…

As my son gets ready to finish up his last year of high school, a season that is so pivotal to the next phase of his life, I am overwhelmed with hit after hit. Navigating this season has been so complicated because he is trying to discover what his purpose is in life, and here I am questioning if I can continue to walk in my own.

The Rush of Milestones

Senior year. Just saying it feels surreal.

College emails, scholarship applications, final yearbook photos, cap and gown orders, driving—everything is moving so fast. And in the midst of it all, I'm doing my best to stay grounded. As my son begins this final stretch of high school, I feel the weight of making sure I help him transition well. I want to support his dreams, guide his choices, and be present for every moment; while still managing everything else life demands.

But there's more to this season for me. When I look at him preparing to walk across a graduation stage, I'm also reminded of where *my* journey began. I was 17 when I got pregnant with him. I was in my own senior year, filled with fear, unknowns, and what felt like a world of impossibilities. And now here I am, watching the very child I once carried grow into a young man preparing to step into his own future. It's a full-circle moment that's both beautiful and emotionally complex.

I remember when the brochures and deadlines started pouring in. I'd look at them and think, *Am I ready for this? Did I give enough of myself to prepare him for what's next?* The sigh in my head is loud every time another decision comes through, but I keep offering my son a steady smile. Meanwhile, I'm whispering prayers under my breath, *Lord, help me lead him well without losing myself in the process.*

Balancing Purpose and Pressure

There's so much pressure to get it right. Not just for him…but for me, too.

I'm still a woman called to walk in purpose. I still have assignments, responsibilities, and dreams that tug at me daily. I've learned the hard way that your calling doesn't stop just because you're navigating a demanding season of motherhood. God doesn't revoke purpose when life gets full, He refines it.

The challenge has been learning how to lead while releasing. How to guide my son forward while not falling behind in my own journey. Some days, I feel like I'm balancing on a wire—steadying purpose in one hand and parenting in the other. It's a sacred juggle that no one fully sees. But

I feel it in my body. I feel it in my spirit. And still, I choose to show up for both.

There are moments when I wonder if I've missed something—some part of *me*—because I've been so committed to pouring into him. But then I remember: motherhood and mission were never meant to cancel each other out. They can coexist, even if they don't always look perfect. Even if one feels heavier than the other some days.

The Public Yes in a Private Stretch

Before senior year even began, I said yes to leading the *Moments for Moms: Legacy Unlocked* Conference. That yes wasn't convenient—it was costly. I said yes not because I had everything in order, but because I was being obedient to the call.

I stood in that room, sharing encouragement and vision with other mothers, while wrestling privately with my own questions. I thought saying yes would lead to a rhythm of clarity, confidence, and open doors. But instead, it launched me into a stretch—a refining season where the questions got louder and the answers didn't always come right away.

When will I feel settled again?
When will I stop second-guessing myself as a mother and as a woman of purpose?
When will I see the fruit of all these quiet yeses?

We often think obedience will lead to ease—but in my experience, it often leads to growth. And growth doesn't always feel good. But it's always necessary.

Identity Shift and Turning Point

This season has required me to slow down and re-evaluate where I've been placing my identity. For so long, my life was built around the rhythm of work, motherhood, and survival. Full-time jobs. After-school pick-ups. Late-night emails. Missed moments I longed to experience but couldn't because duty came first.

I wore "busy" like a badge of honor, believing that if I just kept moving, I'd eventually arrive at peace. But God is showing me that purpose isn't about pace—it's about presence. And I don't have to earn my worth through productivity.

As my son begins to prepare for his next chapter, I've found myself asking, *What is God requiring of me now?* Who am I when the house starts to get quieter? When he no longer needs me to wake him up or pack a lunch or walk him through life step by step?

One night, while praying, I heard the Holy Spirit whisper, *"You're not being punished. You're being positioned."* That one sentence shifted everything for me. This isn't the end—it's a divine transition. And I'm not being overlooked—I'm being prepared. I'm not just a mother—I'm a woman still called, still becoming, and still deeply loved by God.

When God Feels Silent but Is Still Moving

Faith in this season hasn't looked like loud declarations or big leaps. It's looked like quiet trust in the in-between. It's looked like praying while driving, journaling in stolen moments, and leaning on God in the exhaustion of it all.

I had to believe that just because God wasn't speaking loudly didn't mean He wasn't moving. I started to recognize Him in the simple things—the peace that settled after hard conversations with my son. The clarity that came in moments of surrender. The strength I didn't even realize I had until I looked back and saw I'd made it through.

He's not just working on my son—He's working on me, too.

A Scripture That Held Me Together

One scripture that grounded me during this season is **Isaiah 30:15**: *"In quietness and confidence shall be your strength."*

This verse gave me permission to breathe. I didn't need to have it all together to be a good mom. I didn't need to have all the answers to walk in purpose. I just needed to trust that God was guiding both of us—me and my son—every single step.

Quietness. Confidence. Strength.
Not through striving, but through surrender.

Words for the Weary Mom

To the mom in a transition season:
I see you. More importantly, *God sees you.*

You are not falling behind—you are being realigned. This stretch doesn't mean you've missed your moment. It means God is making space for your next one.

Don't bury your dreams just because you're raising someone else. Your child's success isn't your finale—it's part of your legacy. You still have chapters left to write. You still have purpose worth pursuing. And you're not behind—you're just being refined.

Gentle Grounding in Purpose

This season has reminded me that transition doesn't mean you lose your purpose—it just means your pace may shift. Give yourself permission to slow down, ask for help, and trust that God is leading you, even when the road ahead feels unfamiliar.

You don't have to choose between parenting and purpose. You can be present for your child and still pursue what God has placed inside of you. Let motherhood sharpen your mission—not silence it.

A few reminders for the quiet, stretching seasons:

- It's okay to be in process while still guiding someone else.
- You can be faithful even when you feel fragile.
- God's grace is sufficient for your pace.
- Showing up imperfectly is still showing up.

Declaration

I declare that I am not forgotten in this season. I am being refined, repositioned, and renewed. I trust that God's timing is perfect, and I choose to walk in confidence, even when the path is quiet. I will not shrink to fit the moment—I will rise with grace, trusting that the One who called me will carry me through.

Refined in the Silence: My Reflection

Juanita Nicole Woodson

Juanita Woodson, a devoted wife and mother, daughter, sister, aunt, and godmother, is the visionary behind the *Moments for Moms* book series—an anthology movement uniting mothers from across the country to share their stories, inspire others, and celebrate every stage of motherhood. At *Moments for Moms*, Juanita believes that every mother's journey is a story worth telling.

Through storytelling, mentorship, and faith-driven encouragement, she empowers mothers to embrace their unique experiences, preserve their legacies, and create meaningful impact in their families and communities. Her mission is to provide a space where moms can share their wisdom, find support, and leave a lasting imprint for generations to come.

Juanita is also the founder of *Moments for Moms: Legacy Unlocked Conference*, a two-day experience designed to empower, inspire, and connect mothers through meaningful conversations and legacy-centered growth. She is the owner of *Grace 4 Purpose Publishing Co.*, where she helps authors bring their stories of faith and purpose to life.

She published her debut book, *Don't Go That Way: Protect Your Purpose*, in 2017, and her most recent release, *Own Your Impact: Strategies for Authors and Entrepreneurs to Establish Authority and Make a Lasting Impact*, continues to expand her mission of empowering others. Juanita is committed to creating spaces where women can protect their purpose, embrace their calling, and create a lasting impact in every area of life.

As the host of the *Authors Impact Hub Podcast* and co-host of the *Hope at the End of the Tunnel Podcast*, she uses her voice to inspire, uplift, and connect with audiences through powerful, purpose-filled conversations. Grounded in faith, family, and legacy, Juanita continues to walk boldly in her God-given purpose—encouraging others to do the same.

Contact Information:

Email: contact@grace4purposeco.com
Instagram: @_juanitanicole_
@authorsimpacthubpodcast
Facebook: Juanita Nicole Woodson
Website: www.grace4purposeco.com

Moments for Moms Volume IV

www.grace4purposeco.com

MOMENTS
for Moms
VOLUME 4

INSPIRATION & WISDOM FOR EVERY
SEASON OF MOTHERHOOD

PRESENTED BY
GRACE 4 PURPOSE PUBLISHING